THE ATLAS OF ECONOMIC INDICATORS

THE ATLAS OF ECONOMIC INDICATORS

A Visual Guide to Market Forces and the Federal Reserve

W. Stansbury Carnes
and Stephen D. Slifer

HarperBusiness
A Division of HarperCollins*Publishers*

Contents

Part I
An Overview

Part II:
The Economic Indicators

Part III
Federal Reserve Operations

Acknowledgements

I'd like to thank several colleagues for invaluable assistance toward the completion of the *Atlas*. Although Steve Slifer had worked independently back in the mid 1980s, the project gained momentum with Fred Fraenkel's suggestion for two internal publications called "By The Numbers." With Jack Rivkin's encouragement, the pamphlets evolved (slowly) into a real book. For the dirty work, kudos go to Ann-Maria Gropp, our talented department editor, and my terrific assistant Elizabeth Macpherson who cranked out a thousand charts and graphs. Intellectual honesty and nit-picking was provided by Shearson senior economists Stan Shipley and Larry Krohn. Many thanks to chief economist Bob Barbera for hiring me in the first place. Finally, I'm grateful to my wife, Mary, who spent many "lost weekends" while I played on the Macintosh.

Stan Carnes

As is always the case, a book cannot emerge without the help of a tremendous number of people. In my case, special thanks go to Cheryl Rubin for many helpful suggestions in the early stages of writing. In addition, Ruth Rogers was extremely willing to make the 18 zillion copies that always seemed to be necessary. But most of all, I owe both thanks and an apology to my wife, Tania, and daughter Katie, who had to endure the numerous nights and weekends when daddy was otherwise engaged.

Steve Slifer

Part I
Overview

1
Market Forces and the Federal Reserve

W hether you are an investor, broker, financial market economist, business student, or speculator, you want to know the future course of the economy and inflation, the likely response of the Federal Reserve Bank to these developments, and, finally, the implications for interest rates. Why are we all so interested? Simply because the combination of these factors is going to largely determine the direction of the major financial markets.

This book is a simple, easy-to-use pictorial guide to the economic indicators and the Federal Reserve — the primary factors that move the markets. It describes how these key indicators work and what effect they have, and takes a detailed look at the U.S. central bank. Using this book as a guide, you will be better able to interpret the reactions of financial markets to economic news and plan accordingly.

FIXED-INCOME MARKETS ARE DIRECTLY LINKED TO INTEREST RATES

Our first look is at the fixed-income markets. These markets are inexorably linked to interest rates because of the inverse relationship that exists between interest rates and the price of a security. When interest rates rise, the price of a bond falls and vice versa *(Fig. 1-1)*. For example, suppose an investor holds a Treasury bond that yields 8.0%. If the economy expands rapidly, inflation will eventually begin to climb — pushing bond yields higher to, say, 10.0%. In that case, the 8.0% bond will become less attractive and its price will decline; investors would rather own the new higher yielding 10.0% security. Thus, any market force that causes the economy to grow more rapidly, or causes the inflation rate to rise, increases the likelihood that the Federal Reserve will raise interest rates and decrease prices in the fixed-income markets *(Fig. 1-2)*. Similarly, the process works just as well in reverse. Any market force that causes economic activity to decline, or the inflation rate to drop, increases the likelihood that the Federal Reserve will lower interest rates and raise prices in the fixed-income markets. Since the prices of fixed-income securities are so closely linked to interest rates, it is crucial for participants in this market to be cognizant of developments in the economy, the pace of inflation, and implications for Federal Reserve policy.

Figure 1-1 How Bond Yields and U.S. Treasury Security Prices Are Related

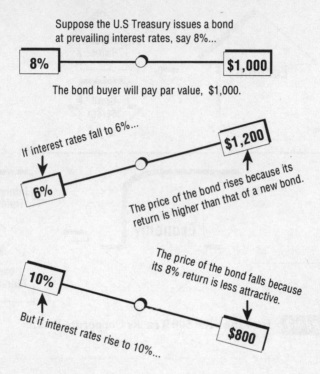

Suppose the U.S Treasury issues a bond at prevailing interest rates, say 8%...

8% ———————O——————— $1,000

The bond buyer will pay par value, $1,000.

If interest rates fall to 6%...

6% $1,200

The price of the bond rises because its return is higher than that of a new bond.

The price of the bond falls because its 8% return is less attractive.

10%

But if interest rates rise to 10%...

$800

THE STOCK MARKET IS TIED TO CORPORATE PROFITS — PLUS THE ECONOMY, INFLATION, AND INTEREST RATES

Movements in the equity (or stock) market are directly linked to the outlook for corporate profits. If profits are expected to rise, then stock prices will also rise. As you can see from *Figure 1-3,* when times are good and corporate profits are rising, the stock market also rises. But, when bad times hit and corporate profits drop (such as in the recessions of 1973-74 and, again, in 1980-82), the stock market also falls. This relationship seems very sensible if you think about what determines corporate profits. Quite clearly the pace of economic activity plays a major role *(Fig. 1-4).* If the economy dips into recession, corporate profits are certain to slide —

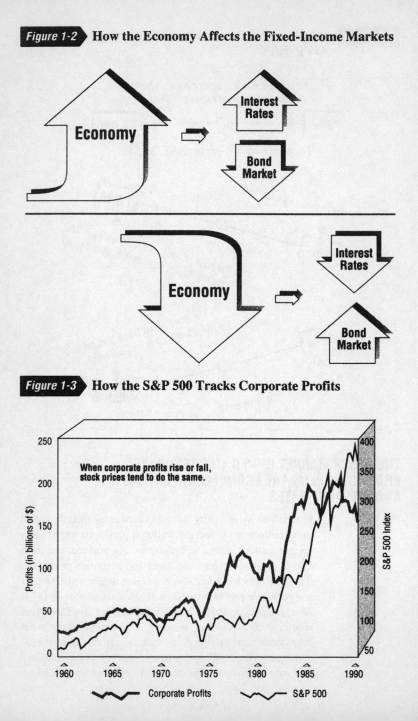

Figure 1-2 How the Economy Affects the Fixed-Income Markets

Figure 1-3 How the S&P 500 Tracks Corporate Profits

When corporate profits rise or fall, stock prices tend to do the same.

How the Macroeconomy Affects Corporate Profits and Stock Prices

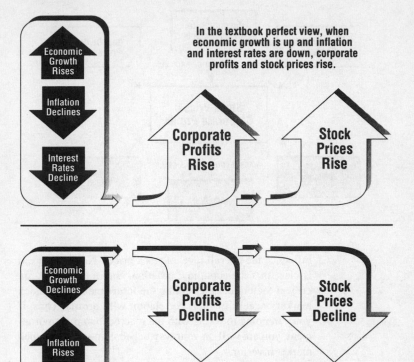

In the textbook perfect view, when economic growth is up and inflation and interest rates are down, corporate profits and stock prices rise.

Similarly, in the textbook perfect view, when economic growth is down and inflation and interest rates are up, corporate profits and stock prices decline.

clearly a negative event for the stock market. Inflation also plays a role. To the extent that inflation rises, the real value of earnings and dividends declines — usually prompting stock prices to fall. Thus, a pickup in inflation is also viewed negatively by the equity markets. And if interest rates rise, the increased cost of borrowing by corporations reduces earnings. There is no question that other factors can play a role in establishing stock prices *(Fig. 1-5)*. At the micro level, management changes, technological developments, and the implementation of more sophisticated cost control procedures are important in determining the price of an individual company's stock. And, if the company is large enough, it can

Figure 1-5 Factors Affecting the Stock Market

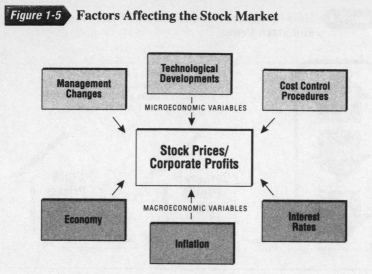

influence the overall level of stock prices. Nevertheless, it is clear that the economy, inflation, and interest rates are critical factors in determining the future path of the stock market because of their correlation with profits. Thus, if you can come to terms with the macroeconomic environment, you are well on your way to becoming a better stock market investor.

THE DOLLAR DEPENDS ON U.S. INTEREST RATES RELATIVE TO OVERSEAS RATES

Similarly, the foreign exchange markets are influenced by what is happening to the U.S. economy, inflation, and interest rates. *Figure 1-6* indicates that interest rates and the value of the dollar are linked. Specifically, the chart compares the difference, or spread, between interest rate levels on 10-year government bonds in the United States and Germany to the exchange rate between the dollar and the German deutschmark. As the spread widens — that is, as the interest rate levels in the United States are rising relative to rates overseas — the dollar rises. The reason for this relationship is that interest-rate differentials are important ingredients in determining where investors are going to place their funds. If interest rates

Rate Spreads Between the United States and Other Countries Can Have an Impact on the Dollar

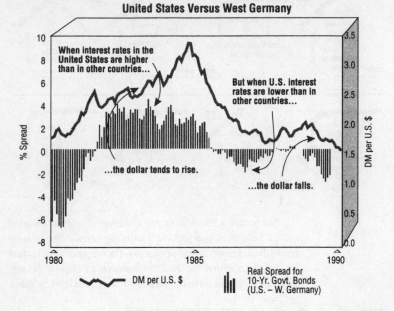

United States Versus West Germany

When interest rates in the United States are higher than in other countries...

But when U.S. interest rates are lower than in other countries...

...the dollar tends to rise.

...the dollar falls.

— DM per U.S. $

Real Spread for 10-Yr. Govt. Bonds (U.S. – W. Germany)

in the United States rise relative to foreign rates, dollar investments become more attractive *(Fig. 1-7)*. This heightened interest in U.S. securities means that foreign investors will need more dollars to make those purchases, hence the dollar tends to rise. Similarly, if U.S. interest rates decline in comparison with rates overseas, foreign securities are preferable and the value of the dollar declines. Of course, other factors can be important at times. For example, in 1985, U.S. policymakers decided that the greenback was overvalued and tried to actively push the value of the dollar lower via intervention in the foreign exchange markets. Events overseas can be important as well. The strength of the Japanese and German economies, their inflation rates, and the direction of their interest rates are equally important. But there is no question that the pace of economic activity in the United States, our inflation rate, and our interest rates greatly influence the value of the dollar.

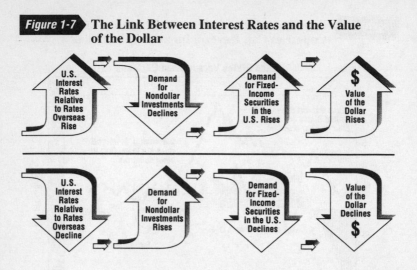

Figure 1-7 The Link Between Interest Rates and the Value of the Dollar

No matter what market you are most closely associated with, it behooves you to have a working knowledge of what drives the economy, what produces inflation, and what factors are going to cause the Federal Reserve to change policy. Ultimately, you need to forecast the direction of interest rates.

GNP = C + I + G + X – M (OR CONSUMPTION + INVESTMENT + GOVERNMENT EXPENDITURES + EXPORTS – IMPORTS)

We have found that most market participants have a reasonably good theoretical knowledge of the economy and how it functions. Yet, these same market participants seem to have difficulty interpreting the series of economic indicators that are released each month and figuring out the implications for the economy or inflation. And who would not? Back in that Economics 101 class, you learned that GNP represents the sum of consumption spending, investment, government expenditures, and exports minus imports (or the old GNP = C + I + G + X – M equation) which is shown pictorially in *Figure 1-8*. It turns out that almost every one of the economic indicators fall into one of these categories, and each one is useful for the information it provides about the overall economy. We will consider, for example, where construction spending fits into this framework, what the purchasing managers' report means, and try to sort through the employment report. When we

Figure 1-8 **Gross National Product Components**

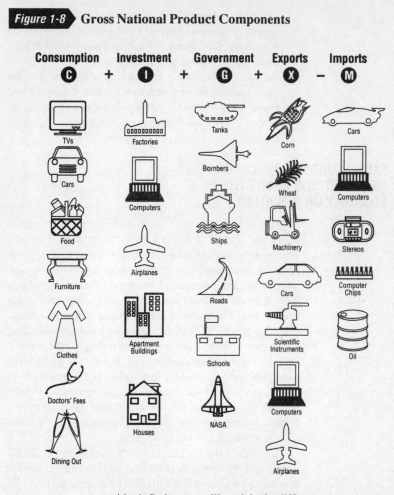

consider inflation, we will explain the difference between the implicit price deflator, the fixed-weight deflator, the CPI, and the PPI, and what you should expect when one of these numbers is released.

The first part of the book deals with the various economic indicators. For each series we want to focus on three things:

» *What the indicator means.* Why do we care what happens to it? What does it tell us about the economy? What does it tell us about inflation, about interest rates, about the Federal Reserve's policy? What other things are important about this indicator?

>> *The background of each indicator*. Who publishes the series? When is it released? How reliable is it? How do economists form their expectations about what that indicator will do for any given month?

>> *The market's response to each indicator*. How will the fixed income markets react to a higher-than-expected figure for GNP growth? What will happen to the equity markets? What will happen to the foreign exchange markets?

EACH ECONOMIC INDICATOR TELLS US SOMETHING ABOUT THE ECONOMY OR INFLATION

As mentioned earlier, each economic indicator is associated with a part of the GNP = C + I + G + X – M equation *(Fig. 1-9)*. The construction spending indicator referred to above, for example, falls under the "I" category as it provides us with information about residential and nonresidential spending — both of which are important parts of the investment component of GNP. The construction spending report is also included under the "G" category because it tells us something about state and local government spending. Some reports, such as the monthly employment report, the purchasing managers' survey, leading indicators, and quarterly GNP, tell us nothing about the various components of GNP. Rather, these reports tell us about GNP itself. They are broader indices that more appropriately apply to the economy as a whole, and not to its parts.

Some indicators — such as the PPI, the CPI, and the fixed-weight and implicit price deflators — do not refer to what is happening with GNP, but to inflation. Later in the text, we will highlight the differences between these various inflation measures and the advantages and disadvantages of each.

As we noted at the outset, any market indicator that points towards a faster pace of GNP growth or higher inflation is generally regarded as a negative for the fixed-income markets because it implies higher interest rates and, hence, lower bond prices. Similarly, once you understand what is happening to the economy and what that suggests for interest rates, the appropriate response of the equity and foreign exchange markets can be determined.

Figure 1-9 The GNP Formula

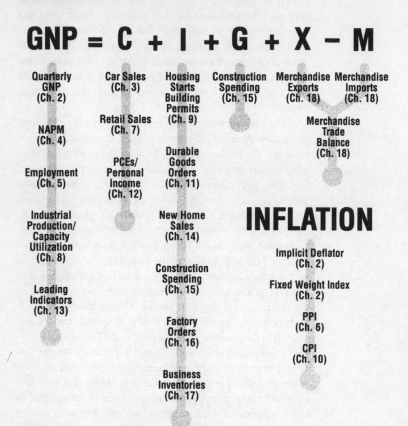

THE MARKET REACTS WHEN THE ACTUAL CHANGE OF AN INDICATOR DIFFERS FROM THE MARKET CONSENSUS

While it is clearly important to understand what an indicator tells us about the economy or inflation, it is also extremely important to recognize that the market's reaction is going to be determined more by how it compares to the market's consensus forecast than by the absolute change in an indicator. For example, suppose that the market believes that GNP growth for some particular quarter is going to rise only 0.5%. If the Commerce Department data reveal that growth was actually 1.0%, the fixed-income markets probably will decline because GNP was more rapid than had been expected, *even though* a 1.0% growth rate is still quite slow. The equity markets probably will also decline because the higher-than-anticipated GNP advance reduces the likelihood that the Federal Reserve will ease monetary policy and, hence, interest rates may not decline in the near future.

The employment report for May 1990 is a classic example of how the markets react to a figure that is different than expected. On Friday, June 1st, the Bureau of Labor Statistics reported an increase in payroll employment for May of 164,000. The street consensus was for a gain of about 200,000. In addition, the April rise in payroll was revised downward from an *increase* of 64,000 initially, to a *decline* of 23,000. The combination of a smaller than expected increase for May *and* a sharp downward revision to April increased the likelihood that the Federal Reserve would ease in the relatively near future and that interest rates would decline. As a result, the bond market rose by nearly two points the same day, causing the yield on 30-year bonds to decline 16 basis points from 8.58% to 8.42%. The stock market also reacted to the prospect of lower rates — the Dow Jones Industrial average rose 24 points, closing above 2900 for the first time. The point is simply that the market's short-term reaction is determined by whether a number is higher or lower than expected, rather than by the absolute value of the number. In our discussion of each indicator, we try to include several factors that economists look at in order to make forecasts. The sum of these views becomes the street's "consensus" — the benchmark by which a number is deemed to be stronger or weaker than expected.

AN INDICATOR'S VALUE IS PARTLY DETERMINED BY ITS RELEASE DATE

It is also important to understand that an indicator's value is determined, to some extent, by its release date. With the exception of the GNP report, which is presented first because it is so important, our discussion of the various economic statistics is presented in chronological order for a typical month. We have ranked the importance of each using a "star" system whereby:

☆☆☆☆ = **crucially important**
☆☆☆ = **usually important**
☆☆ = **occasionally important**
☆ = **routine**

Figure 1-10 provides you with a list of the indicators' approximate release dates. The first hard data that we receive each month are car sales, released shortly after the end of each ten day period. Those data are followed closely by the purchasing managers' report. And then, on the first Friday of each month,

Figure 1-10 Release Dates for Economic Indicators

Report	Chapter	Release Date
Car sales	Ch. 3	13th, 23rd of same month; 3rd of following month
Purchasing managers' report	Ch. 4	1st business day of following month
Employment	Ch. 5	1st - 7th of following month
PPI	Ch. 6	9th - 16th of following month
Retail sales	Ch. 7	11th - 14th of following month
Industrial production/ Capacity utilization	Ch. 8	14th - 17th of following month
Housing starts/ Building permits	Ch. 9	16th - 20th of following month
CPI	Ch. 10	15th - 21st of following month
Durable goods orders	Ch. 11	22nd - 28th of following month
GNP	Ch. 2	21st - 30th of following month
Personal income/ Consumption spending	Ch. 12	22nd - 31st of following month
Leading indicators	Ch. 13	Last business day of following month
New home sales	Ch. 14	28th - 4th for two months prior
Construction spending	Ch. 15	1st business day for two months prior
Factory orders	Ch. 16	30th - 6th for two months prior
Business inventories/sales	Ch. 17	13th - 17th for two months prior
Merchandise trade deficit	Ch. 18	15th - 17th for two months prior

we view the employment report — providing our first fairly complete sense of what happened to the economy during the prior month. A week later, the producer price index (PPI), retail sales figures, and industrial production data are released. This continues until several weeks later when we receive data on business inventories and the merchandise trade deficit — invariably the last indicators for any given month. There is no question that information released *first* is much more valuable than the *last* data to be published, simply because the new information tells us something that we did not know previously. When we have already seen 16 indicators for a given month, what marginal value do the 17th and 18th indicators have? Not a lot. By the time the last indicators are published, we are anxious to see what happened in the following month.

IF AN INDICATOR IS EXTREMELY VOLATILE, ITS VALUE IS REDUCED

One final point concerning the indicators should be noted — the *theoretical* importance of an indicator is not always the same as its *actual* value. A classic example is the orders data. Theoretically, if one knows what is happening to orders, and whether the stack of orders on a manager's desk is growing or shrinking, one should be able to make some inference about what is likely to happen to production in the months ahead. But, unfortunately, the orders data are extremely volatile *(Fig. 1-11)*. If an aircraft order of $3 billion happens to be included in one month's data, durable goods orders can rise by three percentage points in that month. The next month when orders return to normal, durables will decline by 3.0%. Because of these exaggerated swings, it is difficult to attach a great deal of weight to a single month's data point. Thus, for some types of reports, it's better to take a three-month moving average which helps to smooth the data — and tells us whether there has been a significant change in trends.

HOW THE FEDERAL RESERVE *DETERMINES* AND *IMPLEMENTS* MONETARY POLICY

After reading Part II of this book, investors will have a better sense of the information that each economic indicator

Figure 1-11 **Durable Goods Orders: Month-to-Month Versus Three-Month Moving Average**

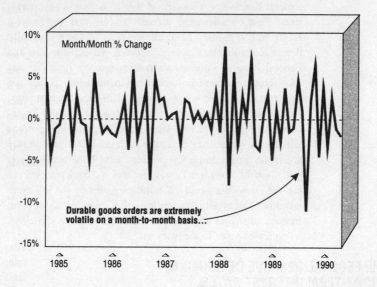

Month/Month % Change

Durable goods orders are extremely volatile on a month-to-month basis...

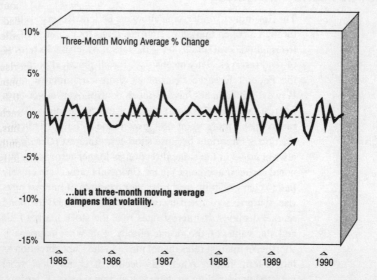

Three-Month Moving Average % Change

...but a three-month moving average dampens that volatility.

conveys about the state of the economy or inflation and, more importantly, what these indicators tell us about the future direction of interest rates. Part III of this book deals with the Federal Reserve and its critical role in determining interest rates. First, we describe the crucial role that the Federal Reserve plays in influencing interest rates, and how it actually determines monetary policy. Second, we explain how the Federal Reserve controls short-term interest rates but not long-term rates, and how changes in monetary policy are transmitted to the economy through changes in interest rates. Finally, we explain how the Federal Reserve actually implements that policy. There are several steps to this process which can sometimes be rather technical. But you should spend the time reading this portion of the book because you will discover how monetary aggregates and bank reserves are related, how the level of borrowings from the discount window essentially determines the level of short-term interest rates, and how the Federal Reserve sends signals of its policy changes to the markets.

THE FEDERAL RESERVE DETERMINES SHORT-TERM INTEREST RATES, BUT NOT LONG-TERM RATES

The first thing to understand about the Federal Reserve is that, through its open market operations, it has total control of the overnight federal funds rate — the rate at which banks borrow or lend reserves. This means that, for all practical purposes, the Federal Reserve determines short-term interest rates. However, it does not have as much control over longer-term interest rates such as bond yields or mortgage rates — those rates depend more upon GNP growth and inflation. This distinction is important because short-term interest rates *do not* always move in the same direction as longer-term rates. We noted earlier that changes in the financial markets are closely tied to changes in interest rates. For example, if interest rates rise, the prices of fixed-income securities fall and the bond market declines. If interest rates rise, the stock market falls and the value of the dollar climbs. But what happens if short-term interest rates do not move in the same direction as longer-term rates? When this occurs, it is not clear what investment or trading strategy you should pursue. Therefore, you must be aware not only of what is happening to the economy and the inflation rate, which largely determine the direction of *longer-term* interest rates, but also of what the Federal Reserve is doing. For all practical purposes, the Federal Reserve determines *short-term* interest rates. What this really means is that you, as a market participant, must be aware of the shape of the *yield curve* — which shows interest rate levels for different maturities.

As an example of how short-term and long-term interest rates can move in different directions, *Figure 1-12* shows the yield curve at two different points in time. The bottom curve is the one that existed in early January 1990 when the bond

Figure 1-12 Federal Reserve Policy, Longer-Term Interest Rates, and Market Psychology

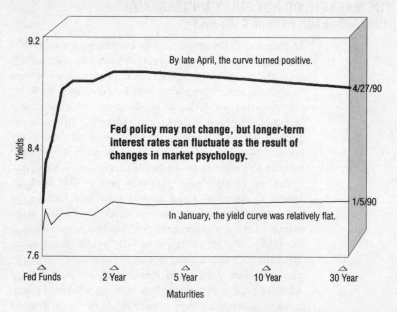

market was very bullish and interest rates were expected to decline further. The Federal Reserve, at that time, pegged the funds rate at almost exactly 8.25%. But the markets were convinced that the economy was heading into a recession and that inflation would recede. This extremely favorable market psychology pushed long-dated bond yields to 8.04%, or 21 basis points (or hundredths of a percent) *below* the funds rate. A few months later, the world turned topsy-turvy as the economic data suddenly became much stronger and oil prices surged. At that point, the Federal Reserve still wanted the funds rate around 8.25%. However, the apparent strength in the economy, by this time, had pushed inflationary expectations much higher, and bonds yields climbed to 9.0% or 75 basis points *higher* than the funds rate. Throughout this period Federal Reserve policy was unchanged, as evidenced by the fact that the funds rate remained at 8.25%. Yet the dramatic change in market psychology caused bond yields to rise by a full percentage point. Clearly, the Federal Reserve essentially "targets" the funds rate, but the economy and inflationary expectations are the driving forces behind longer-term interest rates.

THE MARKETS DO NOT FULLY UNDERSTAND HOW MONETARY POLICY WORKS

Many traders, salespeople, and investors have a good understanding of the *theoretical* aspects of monetary policy. They know that, as shown in *Figure 1-13,* the Federal Reserve tries to regulate money supply growth by controlling bank reserves, and they recall that, by regulating growth in the money supply, the Federal Reserve can indirectly influence the pace of economic activity and the inflation rate. Many people, however, become confused because they do not fully understand how the Federal Reserve uses open market operations to *implement* monetary policy. This book attempts to clarify this and answer questions such as the following: Why does the Federal Reserve intervene in the market every day doing repos or matched sales? What is the importance of a coupon or bill "pass?" What is the difference between a customer and system repo? How can you tell when the Federal Reserve is changing policy? Also, we hope to explain the link between what the Federal Reserve is doing in theory — controlling the growth rate of bank reserves — and the direct effect that has on short-term interest rates. As we will soon see, this link is crucial.

Figure 1-13 Federal Reserve Policy: Theory Versus Reality

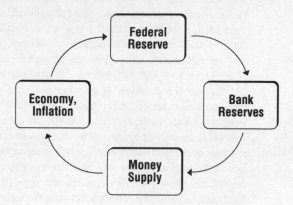

This is the way people think monetary policy works.

Federal Reserve

Bank Reserves

Money Supply

Economy, Inflation

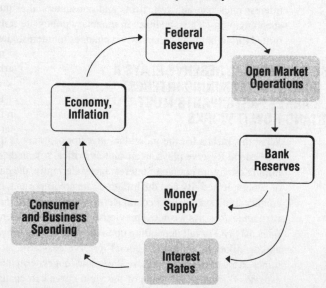

This is the way it really works.

Federal Reserve

Open Market Operations

Bank Reserves

Interest Rates

Money Supply

Consumer and Business Spending

Economy, Inflation

THE FEDERAL RESERVE TRANSMITS POLICY CHANGES TO THE ECONOMY VIA CHANGES IN INTEREST RATES

Not surprisingly, you will find that — like the rest of us — Federal Reserve officials look at the economic indicators, the inflation rate, the value of the dollar, and the conditions in the financial markets before making policy decisions. These factors are all detailed in the minutes of each Federal Open Market Committee (FOMC) meeting. If the Federal Reserve decides that the economy is growing too rapidly and the inflation rate is unacceptably high, it will move to tighten monetary policy. In the *theoretical* world, this means that the Federal Reserve tries to slow down the growth rate of bank reserves in an effort to moderate growth in the money supply. But in the *real* world, we will find that this process has an immediate effect on short-term interest rates, the federal funds rate in particular. The link between the theoretical and real-world aspects of monetary policy, therefore, is interest rates *(Fig. 1-14)*. By controlling the rate of expansion of bank reserves, the Federal Reserve influences interest rates. As interest rates rise and fall, firms and consumers alter their spending plans. Thus, changes in monetary policy are transmitted throughout the economy via changes in interest rates.

BECAUSE THE FEDERAL RESERVE PLAYS A MAJOR ROLE IN DETERMINING INTEREST RATES, MARKET PARTICIPANTS MUST UNDERSTAND HOW IT WORKS

What this means for the individual investor or trader is that the Federal Reserve plays an absolutely critical role in determining the future course of interest rates. Certainly, the pace of economic activity and the inflation rate are important, but equally significant is the Federal Reserve's response *to these very same data!* As we noted previously, longer-term interest rates may rise or fall depending upon the pace of GNP growth and/or inflation, while the Federal Reserve basically determines short-term rates. As these short- and longer-term interest rates fluctuate, the shape of the yield curve can change.

How the Federal Reserve Puts the Brakes on the Economy

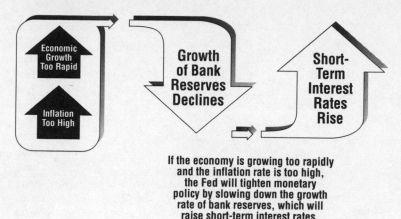

If the economy is growing too rapidly
and the inflation rate is too high,
the Fed will tighten monetary
policy by slowing down the growth
rate of bank reserves, which will
raise short-term interest rates.

However, in general, short- and long-term rates move in the same direction. It is therefore imperative that market participants understand the crucial role played by the U.S. central bank.

ONCE MONETARY POLICY IS DETERMINED, THE FEDERAL RESERVE MUST IMPLEMENT THAT POLICY

In Chapter 21, we show you exactly how the Federal Reserve carries out monetary policy. This is a four-step process which, as we noted earlier, can be rather technical. We are not going to delve into technicalities at this point, but it is worth reading through that portion of the book as there are important lessons to learn at each stage in the process. In that chapter, you will learn how the various money supply measures and bank reserves are related, how the level of borrowing from the discount window determines the funds rate, why the Federal Reserve intervenes in the markets almost every day, and how it sends hints of policy changes to the markets. With this information in hand, you can quickly anticipate the reaction on the part of the financial markets. ✦

Part II
The Economic
Indicators

2

Gross National Product

The Holy Grail of Economics

Importance: ☆ ☆ ☆ ☆

Published by: **Bureau of Economic Analysis, U.S. Department of Commerce**

Availability: **21st – 30th of the month**

Frequency: **Quarterly (revised monthly)**

Volatility: **Moderate**

HOW THE MARKETS REACT:

Fixed-income:
GNP ⇑ ⇒ ⇓ BOND MARKET
GNP ⇓ ⇒ ⇑ BOND MARKET

Equity:
GNP ⇑ ⇒ ⇑ STOCK MARKET
GNP ⇓ ⇒ ⇓ STOCK MARKET

Dollar:
GNP ⇑ ⇒ ⇑ DOLLAR
GNP ⇓ ⇒ ⇓ DOLLAR

NOTEWORTHY CHARACTERISTICS:

✔ This is the most important indicator because it is the broadest measure of economic activity

✔ Virtually all other indicators provide information about this one — Gross National Product.

GNP IS THE MOST IMPORTANT ECONOMIC INDICATOR

ross National Product (GNP) is probably *the* most important report during any given quarter. Real, or inflation-adjusted, GNP is the best single measure of U.S. economic output and spending. Even though GNP is itself one of the economic indicators — which in this book are organized around a typical monthly calendar — we have decided to examine GNP first because it is so crucial. In order to fully appreciate the other economic indicators, you need an overall framework or paradigm. That paradigm is the report on Gross National Product.

Naturally, data contained in the GNP accounts affect the markets because investors, analysts, traders, and economists get a comprehensive sense of where the economy is heading from it. But the GNP reports also influence decisions at the highest levels — from Congressional budget staffers and Federal Reserve policymakers to corporate strategic planners and labor negotiators. When all is said and done, GNP is the figure by which the nation keeps score — not only domestically, but internationally as well.

WHAT IS GNP?

GNP is the sum total of goods and services produced by the United States. Although there are many interpretations (and shortcomings), for our purposes, GNP should be viewed as a measure of demand for U.S. output — the dollar amount spent on a dizzying array of newly produced items. There are four major components included in the GNP accounts: consumption, investment, government purchases, and net exports. In standard macroeconomic parlance, $GNP = C + I + G + (X - M)$ *(Fig. 2-1)*.

CONSUMPTION (C)

The most important sector of the U.S. economy is consumption, or consumer outlays. Economists generally contend that consumption spending represents about two-thirds of GNP. They arrive at this simply by dividing the level of personal consumption expenditures by the level of GNP. How-

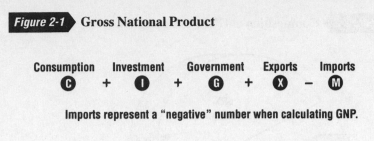

Figure 2-1 **Gross National Product**

Consumption	Investment	Government	Exports	Imports
C	+ **I**	+ **G**	+ **X**	− **M**

Imports represent a "negative" number when calculating GNP.

The GNP calculation can also be illustrated as follows:

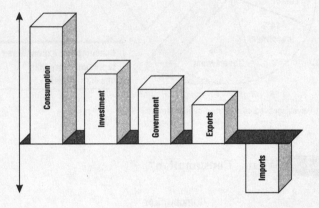

ever, that is not entirely correct. It is important to remember that a portion of consumption spending reflects purchases of imported goods which are not included in GNP. Thus, a more accurate estimate of the consumption component is probably about 56% *(Fig. 2-2)*. Either way, it is clear that the consumption category represents over one-half of GNP, which means it is larger than the other three categories combined. These consumer outlays can be segregated into three categories: durable goods — which are items expected to last three years or more (automobiles, furniture, and golf clubs); nondurable goods — which are expected to last less than three years (food, clothing, and aspirin); and services (medical care, haircuts, and legal fees) *(Fig. 2-3)*. Durable goods account for about 16% of consumption, whereas nondurable goods account for 34% — more than twice as much. Services provide the remaining 50% *(Fig. 2-4)*.

Figure 2-2 ▷ **Composition of GNP: Consumption**

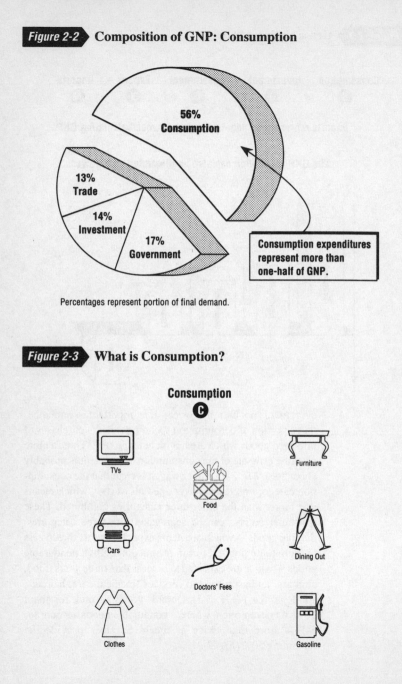

56%
Consumption

13%
Trade

14%
Investment

17%
Government

Consumption expenditures
represent more than
one-half of GNP.

Percentages represent portion of final demand.

Figure 2-3 ▷ **What is Consumption?**

Consumption
C

TVs

Food

Furniture

Cars

Doctors' Fees

Dining Out

Clothes

Gasoline

| Figure 2-4 | **Types of Consumption Spending** |

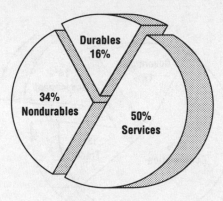

INVESTMENT (I)

Known formally as "gross private domestic investment," investment spending accounts for approximately 14% of GNP *(Fig. 2-5)*. The two broadest categories of investment are nonresidential and residential. The nonresidential component includes spending on plant and equipment (auto factories, computers, and oil rigs). Residential investment is just that: single-family and multi-family home building *(Fig. 2-6)*. The third part of investment spending is the change in business inventories. If inventories are excluded, our GNP estimate will be incorrect. To understand this, it is important to recognize that in calculating GNP we are essentially adding up the dollar amount of goods *purchased* by consumers, businesses, and the government. But GNP represents the amount of goods *produced*. If, for example, General Electric produces 100 refrigerators but sells only 90, its inventory level rises by 10 refrigerators. If we merely add up the amounts spent on goods purchases in that quarter, GNP will be understated — we only counted the 90 refrigerators that were sold. The 10 refrigerators, which were produced but not sold, will *not* be accounted for. Thus, we must incorporate the change in business inventories in our GNP calculation. If inventories are rising, the rise in business inventories is *added to* GNP. If inventories are falling, the fall in business inventories is *subtracted from* GNP.

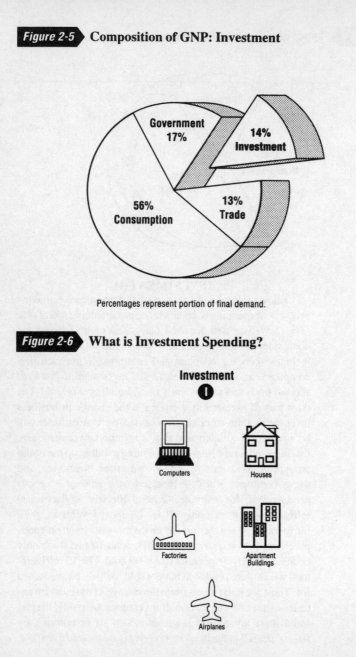

Figure 2-5 **Composition of GNP: Investment**

Percentages represent portion of final demand.

Figure 2-6 **What is Investment Spending?**

GOVERNMENT (G)

The next component of GNP is "G," or government spending. As you are well aware, the government spends a lot of money. While the benefits are sometimes debatable, the Commerce Department assumes that the government's outlays count toward the GNP totals. In other words, government purchases of nuclear weapons, tanks, and highways end up as income for someone *(Fig. 2-7).* Government spending —

Figure 2-7 **What is Included in Government Spending?**

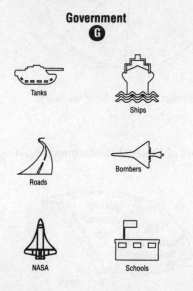

Government
G

Tanks

Ships

Roads

Bombers

NASA

Schools

federal, state, and local — accounts for approximately 17% of GNP *(Fig. 2-8).* Federal spending is roughly 42% of total government expenditures. The major categories in the federal budget are entitlements (Social Security, Medicare, and veterans benefits), 45%; defense (aircraft carriers, bombs, and tanks), 25%; "discretionary" spending (NASA, the Park Service, the IRS, and the FBI), 16%; and interest payments, 14% *(Fig. 2-9).*

Figure 2-8 ▶ Composition of GNP: Government

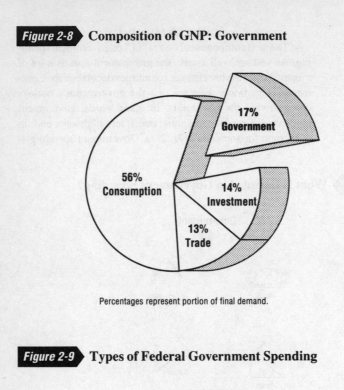

Percentages represent portion of final demand.

Figure 2-9 ▶ Types of Federal Government Spending

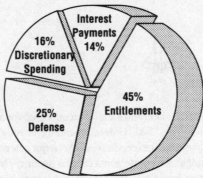

NET EXPORTS (X – M)

By all rights, the final component of GNP should be referred to as "net imports," instead of the traditional textbook definition of "net exports," since the United States has not experienced a surplus of exports over imports in quite some time. In any case, exports *add* to GNP because these goods and services are produced here, and imports *subtract* from GNP because they are produced by a foreign country or overseas firm. The principal goods that we export and import are shown on *Figure 2-10*. The importance of the trade sector has in-

Figure 2-10 **What the United States Exports and Imports**

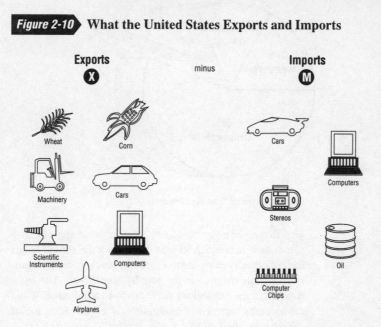

creased in recent years, and it now represents about 13% of total spending in the economy *(Fig. 2-11)*. The United States currently runs a huge deficit on goods and services (that is, X – M is negative), in the amount of $90 billion per year in current dollars. It should be noted here that the "market-moving" monthly trade figures reflect merchandise only. In the quarterly GNP report, the U.S. net export balance includes services and "invisibles," such as freight, insurance, and so forth. (See Chapter 18 for more details.)

A LOOK BACK

What is the long-run track record of the U.S. economy? What constitutes above-average growth? How do we define a recession? These are some of the questions we discuss in this section. As *Figure 2-12* demonstrates, the average sustainable

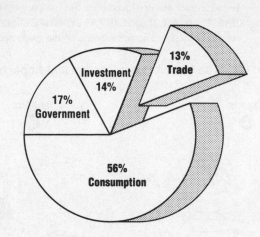

| Figure 2-11 | Composition of GNP: Trade

Percentages represent portion of final demand.

growth rate for inflation-adjusted, or real, GNP appears to be somewhere between 2.5% and 3%. While the United States has periodically enjoyed growth rates in excess of 6%, expansions of this magnitude are usually short-lived. The main reason that the expansions are short-lived is inflation. When the economy is growing rapidly, firms — experiencing robust demand for their products and services — invariably raise prices. At some point, price gains begin to exceed wage increases thereby halting the consumer's ability to spend. Or, if the consumer continues to spend with borrowed money, the Federal Reserve tightens monetary policy — the resulting higher interest rates bring an end to business investment and consumer debt expansion. Usually, some of each scenario takes place and the boom is brought to a close.

In an economic downturn, known as a recession, the reverse is true: there is insufficient demand from consumers, business, and government to sustain activity. On at least seven occasions since World War II, the U.S. economy has slipped into recession — defined as two consecutive quarters when real GNP is negative. The most recent recessions occurred in the 1974-75, 1980-82, and 1990-91 periods.

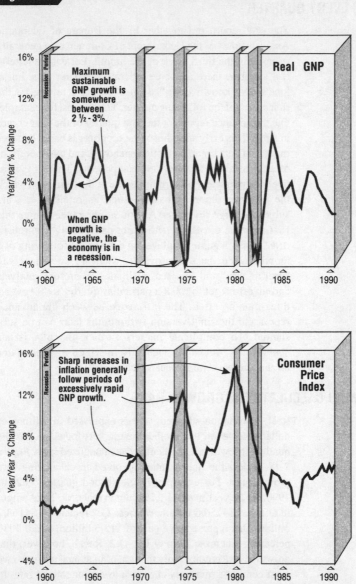

Figure 2-12 How Real GNP Affects Inflation

Real GNP

Maximum sustainable GNP growth is somewhere between 2 ½ - 3%.

When GNP growth is negative, the economy is in a recession.

Consumer Price Index

Sharp increases in inflation generally follow periods of excessively rapid GNP growth.

THERE ARE THREE GNP ESTIMATES
FOR EVERY QUARTER

The GNP report, put together by the Bureau of Economic Analysis (BEA) of the Department of Commerce, is generally released in the third week of the month. For each quarterly GNP number, there are three separate estimates. The initial look at GNP, known as the "advance" report, is released in the first month of the following quarter. This means, for example, that the advance report for the first quarter of the year comes in April. This early snapshot of the economy is based on three months of data for consumption spending, and two months of data for most of the other GNP components. Thus, it is relatively incomplete. Furthermore, some of the figures on which the advance report is based — such as retail sales — are subject to large revisions. As you might expect, since this first estimate of GNP growth is not particularly accurate, a GNP "revision game" is played in each of the following two months when the BEA provides, what are known as, the "preliminary" and "revised" estimates. Therefore, analysts and investors get to track a particular quarter's GNP over a three-month period. The difference between the advance report and the final version two months later can be substantial. To complicate matters further, the BEA issues "benchmark" revisions each July in which it recalculates all the numbers going back three years.

HOW TO CALCULATE THE GROWTH RATE

Real, or inflation-adjusted, GNP is expressed in billions of dollars. However, the number the markets focus upon is the quarterly growth rate — calculated at annualized rates. *Figure 2-13* depicts the mathematics involved in calculating GNP growth rates. For example, in the second quarter (Q:2) of 1990, the BEA estimated a 1.2% gain in real GNP. Total output in Q:1 was $4150.6 billion, whereas Q:2 registered $4163.2 billion. This represented a gain of $12.6 billion, or a 0.3036 percentage increase from Q:1 to Q:2. Recall, however, that growth in GNP is commonly thought of in annual terms, so we must convert a quarterly change into an annualized rate. In order to accomplish this you must first divide 4163.2 by 4150.6, which equals 1.003036. Next, raise that number to the fourth power, which is 1.0122. Finally, drop the one in front

How the GNP Revision Game Works

| Advance Estimate | Published in first month of following quarter |

| Preliminary Estimate | Published in second month of following quarter |

| Revised Estimate | Published in third month of following quarter |

| Benchmark Revision | Published the following July (covers the past three years) |

Release Dates for Each GNP Estimate

The First Pass: GNP Advance Estimates

Q1:	April
Q2:	July
Q3:	October
Q4:	January

The Second Pass: GNP Preliminary Estimates

Q1:	May
Q2:	August
Q3:	November
Q4:	February

The Third Pass: GNP Revised Estimates

Q1:	June
Q2:	September
Q3:	December
Q4:	March

and multiply by 100. Voila! The remaining figure is the annual rate of change which, rounded off, equals 1.2%. Fortunately, you need not go through all this — the Bureau of Economic Analysis hands it to you on a silver platter. But now you know their tricks!

There are occasions when you might want to know the growth rate for GNP, or one of its components, and you do not have an official release handy. Or perhaps you do not have a calculator equipped to raise figures to the fourth power. There is an easier way to do all this. Begin in the same manner you

Figure 2-13 How to Calculate GNP Growth Rates

>> **The Hard Way**
(The Commerce Department's method)

$$\left(\frac{Q2}{Q1}\right)^4 - 1 \times 100 = \% \text{ growth rate of GNP}$$

$$\text{or } \left(\frac{4163.2}{4150.6}\right)^4 - 1 \times 100 = 1.2\%*$$

>> **The Easy Way**

$$\left[\left(\frac{Q2}{Q1}\right) - 1\right] \times 4 \times 100 = \% \text{ growth rate of GNP}$$

$$\text{or } \left[\left(\frac{4163.2}{4150.6}\right) - 1\right] \times 4 \times 100 = 1.2\%*$$

*Note: When rounding to only one decimal place,
both methods usually yield the same result.

did previously — divide Q:2 by Q:1, which in this case is 1.003036. This time simply drop the leading "1," multiply by four to annualize the figure (to arrive at .0121), and then multiply by 100 to convert the result into a percent (which brings you to 1.2%).

THE GNP REPORT ALSO CONTAINS INFORMATION ABOUT INFLATION

THE IMPLICIT DEFLATOR MEASURES PRICE CHANGES AND CHANGES IN SPENDING PATTERNS

Along with GNP, the Commerce Department estimates two price deflators — the implicit and fixed-weight deflators — which are actually two different measures of inflation. The implicit deflator is the one cited most often, but it should be noted that it is *not* a pure measure of inflation. Rather, the implicit deflator measures a combination of price changes *and* changes in the composition of GNP. For example, if prices are absolutely unchanged between one quarter and the next, but

GNP is composed of more high-priced goods in the later quarter, the implicit deflator will register an increase *(Fig. 2-14)*. The classic textbook example is the substitution of butter for margarine: if the prices of butter and margarine do not change, but consumers suddenly feel wealthier and start buying more butter and less margarine, the implicit deflator rises. There is now a larger weight given to the higher-priced good. A more up-to-date example occurs in the housing industry: as plumbers substitute relatively inexpensive plastic pipe for more costly copper tubing, the implicit price deflator declines (or at least has a downward bias). Thus, the implicit deflator provides some information about how consumers and firms respond to inflation by changing their

Figure 2-14 How the Fixed-Weight and Implicit Price Deflators Work

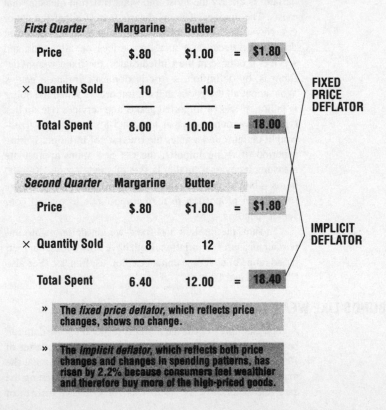

First Quarter	Margarine	Butter	
Price	$.80	$1.00	= $1.80
× Quantity Sold	10	10	
Total Spent	8.00	10.00	= 18.00

Second Quarter	Margarine	Butter	
Price	$.80	$1.00	= $1.80
× Quantity Sold	8	12	
Total Spent	6.40	12.00	= 18.40

FIXED PRICE DEFLATOR

IMPLICIT DEFLATOR

» The *fixed price deflator*, which reflects price changes, shows no change.

» The *implicit deflator*, which reflects both price changes and changes in spending patterns, has risen by 2.2% because consumers feel wealthier and therefore buy more of the high-priced goods.

spending patterns. Certainly, that information is useful. In fact, some analysts believe that the deflator is a more relevant concept than a pure price measure. Keep in mind, however, that the deflator does not tell us precisely what is happening to inflation.

THE FIXED-WEIGHT DEFLATOR TELLS US WHAT IS HAPPENING TO INFLATION

The fixed-weight deflator, on the other hand, is a *pure* measure of inflation. It is not tainted by changes in the composition of GNP. Basically, the Commerce Department takes all the goods that are included in the implicit deflator and holds the market weights constant. As a result, the fixed-weight deflator provides a measure of price changes for an extremely large basket of goods and services — over 5,000 items are included. In terms of coverage, the fixed-weight deflator is clearly the most important inflation measure that exists. The number of items dwarfs that of either the PPI or CPI. Nevertheless, this measure does have some significant drawbacks. Because it measures prices on all goods and services produced in the United States, the fixed-weight deflator is, by definition, a strictly domestic inflation gauge. What about all the goods that are imported? When the dollar is falling, prices of imported goods and services rise. In this type of environment, as in the 1985-86 period, the fixed-weight deflator understates the true rate of inflation. During a period of rising imports, the CPI is a more appropriate measure. It covers a smaller basket of goods — only 300-400 items — but it has the advantage that imported goods are included in proportion to their importance in overall consumer spending.

In sum, the implicit and fixed-weight deflators are important measures of inflation. Both have drawbacks, but their broad range of coverage enhances their usefulness. (See also Chapters 6 and 10.)

BONDS LIKE WEAK GNP GROWTH

A good example of how the markets respond to GNP data can be found in the 1.2% growth rate for the second quarter of 1990 *(Fig. 2-15)*. As usual, it is important to note what the market was expecting. The consensus view approaching the data release of July 27, 1990 was for Q:2 GNP growth of approximately 1.8%. Not only was the actual pace lower than anticipated, but the Commerce Department simultaneously released benchmark revisions going back to 1987. (Recall that, in July, the benchmark revisions covering the previous three years are released.) Instead of a 1989 growth rate of 2.6%, the Department said it was only 1.8%. Moreover, GNP for the first quarter of 1990 dropped to 1.7% from 1.9%. All this was wonderful news for the bond market — the 30-year Treasury bond yield fell to 8.48% from the prior day's close of 8.55%. By the following day, the yield was down to 8.41%. Short-term rates fell as well. We will see again and again that sluggish growth is taken positively by the fixed-income markets.

Figure 2-15 **Market Reaction to GNP**

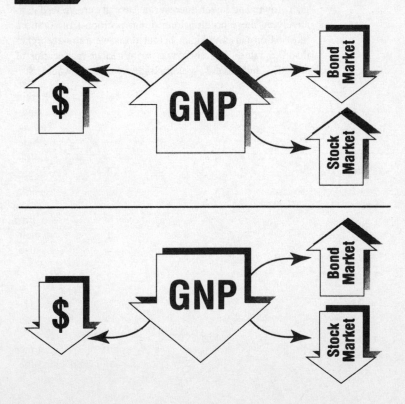

STOCKS DO NOT

In this example, the GNP news was not well received by the stock market. There had been worries, for some time, that the economy was flirting with a recession and that corporate profits had been sinking for months. The equity market was not pleased to hear that growth was even lower than anticipated. Sometimes the stock market shrugs off indications of weak GNP — if interest rates decline significantly in an environment of decent profits. On this occasion, however, the DOW headed south by some 22 points.

NEITHER DOES THE DOLLAR

For the dollar, the new information was bearish. With inflation still relatively high — and with a perception lurking that the Federal Reserve would be forced to ease credit anyway — the greenback declined against most major currencies. Sluggish growth and lower interest rates usually are viewed negatively by those holding long dollar positions. In addition, rates in Germany and Japan, in real terms, were already higher than U.S. rates. Thus, there was an immediate reallocation of so-called "hot money" seeking higher yields elsewhere. ⬥

3
Car Sales
The First Hint

Importance:	☆ ☆
Published by:	**Automobile manufacturers**
Availability:	**Three business days after the end of the period**
Frequency:	**Every 10 days (three times per month)**
Volatility:	**Moderate**

HOW THE MARKETS REACT:

Fixed-income:	CAR SALES ⇧ ⇒ ⇩ BOND MARKET
	CAR SALES ⇩ ⇒ ⇧ BOND MARKET
Equity:	CAR SALES ⇧ ⇒ ⇧ STOCK MARKET
	CAR SALES ⇩ ⇒ ⇩ STOCK MARKET
Dollar:	CAR SALES ⇧ ⇒ ⇧ DOLLAR
	CAR SALES ⇩ ⇒ ⇩ DOLLAR

NOTEWORTHY CHARACTERISTICS:

✔ The first piece of economic data released each month.

✔ A leading indicator of economic activity — the first indicator to turn down when the economy goes into recession; the first to rise when it rebounds.

CAR SALES PROVIDE THE FIRST HINT OF ECONOMIC STRENGTH OR WEAKNESS

nit car sales tell us the *number* of cars that were sold during that particular ten day period. This number is useful for several reasons. Most important, it provides the very *first* piece of information concerning the strength or weakness of the economy. The data are released three business days following the end of each ten day period. For example, car sales for the first ten days of March are available around the 13th of March. This means that, prior to the middle of the month, we know what happened to car sales during the first ten day period of that same month. By the 25th of the month, we know what happened in the second ten days. And shortly after month-end, we know what happened for the entire month. No other indicator is as timely because none is released during the course of that same month.

CAR SALES GIVE US CLUES ABOUT OTHER ECONOMIC INDICATORS

Car sales have a second great strength. They can provide us with an important clue concerning the retail sales and personal consumption expenditures (PCE) data to be released later in the month, both of which can be big market movers. Automobile sales represent about 20% of retail sales and about 6% of consumption.

CAR SALES WARN US ABOUT CHANGES IN THE PACE OF GNP GROWTH

Car sales have a third important feature. They can give us an early warning signal of an impending recession, and tell us when we can begin to expect a recovery. The underlying reason is that car sales are very sensitive to changes in interest rates and consumer psychology. If consumers get nervous about the economic outlook, or are bothered by rising interest rates, one of the first things they do is cancel plans to buy a new car. This makes sense because automobiles and housing are obviously the largest expenditures in the family budget. If you are going to cut costs, this is the place to start! Historically, the automobile and housing sectors of the economy are the first to dip into recession when times are bad.

They are also the first sectors to experience a recovery *(Fig. 3-1)*. Thus, car sales tend to be a leading indicator of economic activity, and can provide some clues concerning when the economy is about to change direction. This is why we consider car sales data to be so valuable.

Figure 3-1 ▶ **How Real GNP Traces Auto Sales**

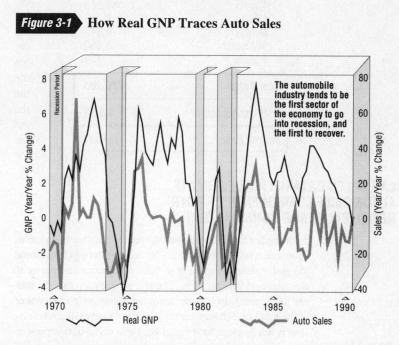

RAW DATA MUST FIRST BE CONVERTED TO ANNUALIZED SELLING RATES

When unit sales data are released for each ten day period of the month, sales for each manufacturer will be published. These raw statistics must be converted to seasonally adjusted annual selling rates to be meaningful, but this is a simple process. The Commerce Department publishes the seasonal factors for the series in advance, which adjust for both seasonal variation and differences in the number of selling days in each period. All you have to do is add up the data for the individual manufacturers and divide by the seasonal factor to see what is happening *(Fig. 3-2)*.

Figure 3-2 Calculating Car Sales Late September 1990

General Motors	102,914
Ford	69,050
Chrysler	27,282
Honda	14,380
Toyota	10,666
Nissan	7,035
Mazda	2,613
Mitsubishi	1,692
Subaru	734

Total Sales	***236,735***

Seasonal Factor	28.93

= | | |
|---|---:|
| ***Selling Rate*** | ***8,183T*** |

CAR SALES DATA HELP TO ESTIMATE AUTOMOBILE COMPONENTS OF BOTH RETAIL SALES AND CONSUMPTION

At the end of a month, when all the car sales data are available, economists take these adjusted figures and attempt to estimate the automobile component of both retail sales and personal consumption expenditures. There is no question that the unit car sales data *help* in estimating the automobile component of the retail sales figure for the month. However, the relationship is not as close as it could be. First, these data represent *unit sales,* which means that we know the number of cars that were sold. In order to link car sales and retail sales, what we really want to know is the *dollar value* of those sales since the retail sales report tells us the dollar amount that was spent on autos and other goods during the course of the month. Second, the automobile component of retail sales also includes used car sales, new and used truck sales, and sales of automobile parts. For these two reasons the relationship between unit car sales and the auto component of retail sales is a loose one.

It is a bit easier to use the unit sales data to estimate the automobile component of personal consumption expenditures because, unlike retail sales, the consumption data do not include used cars *(Fig. 3-3).* In fact, the Commerce Depart-

Figure 3-3 Personal Consumption Expenditures Versus Auto Sales

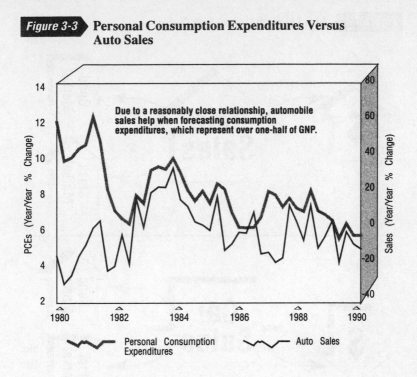

Due to a reasonably close relationship, automobile sales help when forecasting consumption expenditures, which represent over one-half of GNP.

Personal Consumption Expenditures   Auto Sales

ment uses those same data, together with an estimate of the average value of a new car, to come up with their estimate.

CAR SALES CAN MOVE MARKETS

The car sales data are extremely important to the markets because of the following:

» They are timely.

» They help us to estimate other indicators that will be released later in the month.

» They are generally a leading indicator of economic activity.

A stronger-than-expected figure on car sales makes the fixed-income markets jittery since interest rates will rise and bond prices will fall *(Fig. 3-4)*. A more rapid pace of car sales implies faster growth of both the consumption component of GNP and GNP itself. A pickup in the pace of economic activity could induce the Federal Reserve to tighten monetary policy

Figure 3-4 ▶ Market Reaction to Car Sales

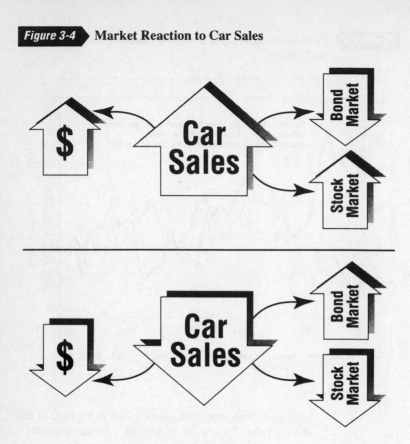

by increasing interest rates. A slower pace of sales would trigger the opposite reaction.

From an equity market point of view, a faster pace of car sales is *usually* a positive event. A pickup in car sales implies a stronger economy which, in turn, leads to higher profits — a plus for the stock market. The exception occurs when market participants believe that the economy is growing too quickly and fear a Federal Reserve tightening. In that instance, the stock market reacts adversely.

What happens to the dollar in the foreign exchange markets depends upon interest rates. If the bond market assumes that the Federal Reserve is going to tighten credit in response to a faster pace of economic activity, the dollar will strengthen. ⬍

4

The Purchasing Managers' Index

A View from the Trenches

Importance: ☆ ☆
Published by: **National Association of Purchasing Management**

Availability: **First business day of the month**
Frequency: **Monthly**
Volatility: **Moderate**

HOW THE MARKETS REACT:

Fixed-income:
NAPM ⇑ ⇒ ⇓ **BOND MARKET**
NAPM ⇓ ⇒ ⇑ **BOND MARKET**

Equity:
NAPM ⇑ ⇒ ⇑ **STOCK MARKET**
NAPM ⇓ ⇒ ⇓ **STOCK MARKET**

Dollar:
NAPM ⇑ ⇒ ⇑ **DOLLAR**
NAPM ⇓ ⇒ ⇓ **DOLLAR**

NOTEWORTHY CHARACTERISTICS:

✔ First complete look at the manufacturing sector.
✔ Tracks the economy fairly well.

THE PURCHASING MANAGERS' INDEX
CORRELATES WELL WITH GNP GROWTH

Always on the lookout for more data, analysts and investors have become hooked on the results of a monthly survey arranged by the National Association of Purchasing Management (NAPM). Released on the first working day of the month, the association's *Report on Business* often provides the first comprehensive look at the manufacturing sector via its "diffusion index" (described below). And since it usually arrives shortly before the all-important employment report (covered later in Chapter 5), the NAPM index is used to fine-tune forecasts of the Bureau of Labor Statistics data. As *Figures 4-1* and *4-2* indicate, the NAPM index tracks the economy's ups and downs fairly well. In fact, many consider this series a valuable adjunct to the Commerce Department's index of leading indicators. As we will see in our upcoming discussion, readings above 50 represent an expanding manufacturing sector, whereas figures below 50 indicate

Figure 4-1 ▶ **How the NAPM Survey Tracks the Economy**

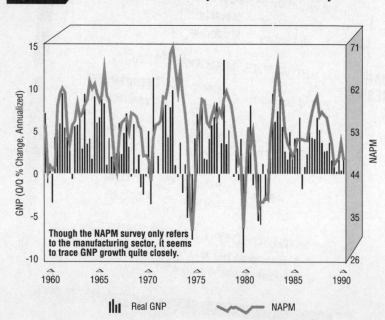

Though the NAPM survey only refers to the manufacturing sector, it seems to trace GNP growth quite closely.

GNP (Q/Q % Change, Annualized)

NAPM

||| Real GNP   〜〜 NAPM

Figure 4-2 **NAPM Versus Leading Indicators**

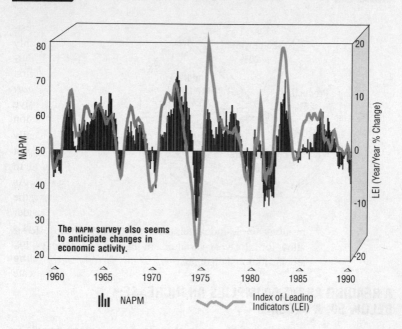

The NAPM survey also seems to anticipate changes in economic activity.

| ╷╷╷ NAPM | Index of Leading Indicators (LEI) |

declining factory activity. The movement away from 50 indicates the magnitude of expansion or decline.

NAPM INDEX IS DERIVED FROM THE RESPONSES TO SIX QUESTIONS

The NAPM survey is valued not only for its timeliness, but also for its information, which is obtained directly from purchasing executives in over 250 industrial companies. Twenty-one industries in 50 states are represented on the Business Survey Committee. Participants respond to a questionnaire regarding production, orders, commodity prices, inventories, vendor performance, and employment by generally characterizing the activity in each category as up, down, or unchanged. For each subgroup a *diffusion index* is formed. The diffusion index is calculated by adding the percentage of positive responses to one-half of those who report conditions as unchanged. Various weights (shown in *Fig. 4-3*) are applied to the individual components to form a composite index. The

Figure 4-3 **Composition of the NAPM Index**

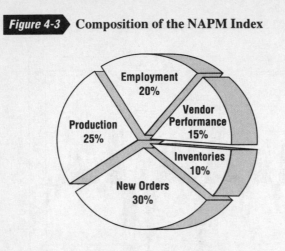

resulting single-index number is then seasonally adjusted to allow for intra-year variations in the weather, holidays, and any institutional changes.

A READING ABOVE 50 IMPLIES AN INCREASE; BELOW 50, A DECLINE

A reading of 50 can be thought of as a "swing point." To understand this, consider the following example. Forget, for the moment, that there are a number of different categories and assume that NAPM asks only one question: "Did orders increase, decrease or remain the same this month?" Let us also assume that *everybody*— 100% of the respondents— reported that orders were unchanged *(Fig. 4-4)*. To calculate the index, we take one-half of the percentage of those who said orders were unchanged ($\frac{1}{2} \times 100 = 50$) and add the percentage of those who said orders increased (zero). Thus, in this example, the orders index would be 50, which means orders were unchanged in that month. A reading above 50 implies an orders increase; a reading below 50 indicates an orders decline. As a rule of thumb, when the NAPM index approaches 60, you can bet investors will begin to worry about the consequences of an overheated economy — higher inflation, bottlenecks, and a Federal Reserve moving in the direction of tighter credit. Conversely, a slide toward 40 strongly suggests that a recession is near at hand. Even though NAPM is basically concerned with manufacturing-type firms, we have

| Figure 4-4 | How NAPM Index is Calculated |

1. If *everybody* agrees that orders were unchanged:

$$
\begin{aligned}
\text{Up} &= 0\% \\
\text{Same} &= 100\% \\
\text{Down} &= 0\%
\end{aligned}
$$

$$\text{NAPM} = (\% \text{ Up}) + \tfrac{1}{2}(\% \text{ same})$$

> *or*   **50** = **0%** + **½ (100%)**

2. If *some* respondents report higher orders:

$$
\begin{aligned}
\text{Up} &= 20\% \\
\text{Same} &= 80\% \\
\text{Down} &= 0\%
\end{aligned}
$$

$$\text{NAPM} = (\% \text{ Up}) + \tfrac{1}{2}(\% \text{ same})$$

> *or*   **60** = **20%** + **½(80%)**

seen that this sector generally leads the overall economy — despite the high (and rising) proportion of services in the U.S. economy.

NAPM IS DIFFICULT TO FORECAST

Unlike other releases, the NAPM index is forecast by only a few economists simply because there is little data upon which to base an educated guess. Those of us who are daring enough to attempt a forecast use information from a similar type survey conducted by the Federal Reserve Bank of Philadelphia — available about two weeks earlier. Also, the Chicago branch of NAPM, one of the association's regional arms, releases the results for the Chicago area one day prior to the national data. These two sources of information provide some clues, but there is still a wide margin for error. Since so few economists make forecasts of this series, and since those who do are frequently humiliated, there is a major "surprise factor" attached to a NAPM release. For that reason, it can sometimes prompt a large market reaction.

IF NAPM RISES, THE BOND MARKET DECLINES

The bond market views strength in the NAPM index as bearish and weakness in the NAPM index as bullish *(Fig. 4-5)*. Of course, one must use some common sense here. If the index

Figure 4-5 Market Reaction to NAPM

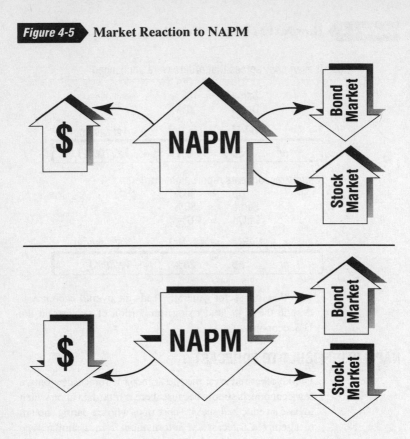

rises to 45.0 in February from 44.0 in January, the bond market is unlikely to fall apart. Remember, the below-50 reading indicates that the manufacturing sector continued to contract in February, but its *rate* of decline was a bit slower in that month because the February reading of 45.0 was higher than the January level of 44.0. Conversely, if interest rates have been trending up along with economic activity, and NAPM rises to 58.0 from 55.0, the bond market quickly reprices — downward.

STOCKS SHOULD IMPROVE

The same logic applies to the stock market. If recent earnings reports have been favorable, and interest rates have been holding steady at relatively low levels, a NAPM index increase can be construed as bullish. However, if other indicators have been suggesting "end-of-cycle" problems — an overheating economy, accelerating inflation, and rising interest rates — a strong index reading will be taken bearishly by the equity market.

AND THE DOLLAR MAY RISE

The dollar takes its cue from the Federal Reserve. If the economy is strong, the U.S. currency rallies on news of advancing manufacturing activity, owing to possible future central bank tightening efforts which would push interest rates higher. Conversely, if the economy is sluggish, the dollar drifts lower on a weak NAPM report because the markets may anticipate that interest rate levels will fall. ❧

5
Employment
The King of Kings!

Importance:	☆ ☆ ☆ ☆ ☆
Published by:	**Bureau of Labor Statistics of the U.S. Department of Labor**
Availability:	**1st – 7th of the month**
Frequency:	**Monthly**
Volatility:	**Payroll Employment – Moderate Unemployment Rate – None**

HOW THE MARKETS REACT:

Fixed-income:

PAYROLL EMPLOY. ⇑ ⇒ ⇓ BOND MARKET
UNEMPLOY. RATE ⇑ ⇒ ⇑ BOND MARKET
PAYROLL EMPLOY. ⇓ ⇒ ⇑ BOND MARKET
UNEMPLOY. RATE ⇓ ⇒ ⇓ BOND MARKET

Equity:

PAYROLL EMPLOY. ⇑ ⇒ ⇑ STOCK MARKET
UNEMPLOY. RATE ⇑ ⇒ ⇓ STOCK MARKET
PAYROLL EMPLOY. ⇓ ⇒ ⇑ STOCK MARKET
UNEMPLOY. RATE ⇓ ⇒ ⇑ STOCK MARKET

Dollar:

PAYROLL EMPLOY. ⇑ ⇒ ⇑ DOLLAR
UNEMPLOY. RATE ⇑ ⇒ ⇓ DOLLAR
PAYROLL EMPLOY. ⇓ ⇒ ⇓ DOLLAR
UNEMPLOY. RATE ⇓ ⇒ ⇑ DOLLAR

NOTEWORTHY CHARACTERISTICS:

✔ The first complete look at the economy for any given month.

✔ Helps to forecast many other economic indicators.

EXCEPT FOR GNP, EMPLOYMENT IS THE MOST IMPORTANT *MONTHLY* ECONOMIC INDICATOR

t has been said that economists never agree on anything. But there may be one exception — the value of the monthly employment report. From our perspective, it represents the single most important report that we get each month. There is no question that the GNP report is the most important economic indicator and, in fact, almost all of the other indicators tell us something about GNP. But GNP is a *quarterly* measure of economic activity (although it is revised monthly). The employment data are monthly and help us refine our GNP estimate for that quarter. Before we view the employment report, we have obtained information on car sales which tells us a bit about retail sales and consumption — but car sales represent less than 5% of GNP. We also have received the purchasing managers' index (NAPM) which gives us a vague idea of what is happening in the manufacturing sector. You will recall that this report tells us whether production, employment, orders, etc., are higher or lower than in the previous month. But other than this generalized feeling for activity in the goods-producing sector, there is no concrete evidence to help analysts and investors refine their forecasts of the economy's direction. Even if we agree that the NAPM is portraying an accurate picture of the manufacturing sector, it is important to recognize that it only represents about 44% of GNP. We know nothing about the construction industry or services, which make up over one-half of our economy, until this report is released. Therefore, no other monthly economic indicator is as important as the employment report.

THIS REPORT PROVIDES INFORMATION ON EMPLOYMENT, AVERAGE WORKWEEK, AND HOURLY EARNINGS

The monthly employment report provides a wealth of information about virtually every sector of the economy. In addition to basic employment statistics for nine major sectors of payroll employment shown in *Figure 5-1*, we discover how many hours people worked in each of those categories (average workweek), and how much they were paid (average hourly earnings). This information is invaluable.

| Figure 5-1 | Major Categories of Payroll Employment |

Goods-Producing
» Manufacturing
» Construction
» Mining

Service-Producing
» Transportation and Public Utilities
» Wholesale Trade
» Retail Trade
» Finance, Insurance, and Real Estate
» Services
» Government

THIS REPORT HELPS ESTIMATE ALMOST EVERY OTHER ECONOMIC INDICATOR

The employment figures are crucial. If we know how many people were employed in the manufacturing sector in a given month, how long they worked, and how much overtime they accrued, it is not too difficult to predict how much they produced — virtually every economist uses this report as one method of estimating industrial production *(Fig. 5-2)*. If, in addition to the above information for all workers, we also know how much these people were paid, we can make a reasonable projection of the change in personal income for that month. The data for the construction industry helps in making a forecast of housing starts. After all, if construction employment surged in a given month, there is a good chance that housing starts also surged. Admittedly, not all of those employed in the construction industry build houses. Some undoubtedly build roads and schools. But there at least is a reasonable correlation between construction employment and starts. Finally, economists use this report to help refine their GNP forecasts for the quarter. GNP is supposed to measure the aggregate volume of good and services produced. If we take the number of jobs and multiply it by the average workweek, we can determine the number of aggregate hours worked for that month. If we perform the same calculation for every

Figure 5-2 **Data from the Employment Report Help Us Forecast Several Other Economic Factors**

month and then average the data for the quarter, we should be able to produce a reasonable GNP estimate. This estimate, however, is not a perfect measure, primarily because productivity changes from one quarter to the next sometimes cause problems. Yet, if productivity is reasonably stable, this method of estimating GNP works well. The point is that the employment report provides us with a wealth of information that we may use in formulating forecasts for many of the other economic indicators released later in the month.

THE UNEMPLOYMENT RATE IS VERY IMPORTANT TO POLITICIANS

The monthly employment report also contains information about the unemployment rate. Because this rate is so politically sensitive, it tends to generate the most press coverage, although from a market viewpoint it is less valuable than the payroll employment data. The reason the unemployment rate is important to the financial markets at all is because the Federal Reserve appears to respond to increases in the unemployment rate. If people are being laid off and the unemployment rate rises, Congressional pressure on the Federal Reserve to ease monetary policy intensifies dramatically.

UNEMPLOYMENT RATE IS A LAGGING INDICATOR OF ECONOMIC ACTIVITY

There is no question that an increase in the unemployment rate is a clear sign that the economy is weak. However, the markets do not pay as much attention to this rate because it is a *lagging* indicator of economic activity, which means that it turns up *after* the economy has peaked and begun to move into a recession, and it begins to fall *after* a recession has ended and the economy, once again, has begun to expand *(Fig. 5-3)*. For example, if firms experience a drop-off in sales activity, the first warning signal is a rise in inventory levels. Firms then try to trim inventories by cutting back on the number of hours their employees work. If sales do not rebound soon and/or inventory levels begin to decline, at some point management will have to consider a cutback in employment. Thus, a rise in the unemployment rate is regarded as a *lagging* indicator of economic activity. This process works equally well in reverse. Companies do not run out and hire additional bodies as their first response to a sales pickup. The sales gain has to be sustained for some period of time. (It should be noted that, in contrast, payroll employment is a *coincident* indicator of economic activity, which means that it changes direction at the *same time* as the economy.)

BEWARE OF REVISIONS

One word of caution: while the payroll employment data are extremely valuable, beware of revisions. In the introduction to this book, we warned that many economic series were subject to sizeable revisions and this is one of them. As an example, the May 1990 data indicated that payroll employment rose 164,000 (which was less than expected), and the April data was revised downward from an initial increase of 64,000 to a decline of 23,000. This weaker-than-expected report caused a major bond market rally; yields on that day dropped by 16 basis points. What is interesting is that a month later, the May gain revised from an increase of 164,000 initially to an astonishing increase of 356,000! This rise sent the bond markets into a tailspin, and over the next two days, yields rose by 15 basis points. In two successive months, revisions to the employment data caused two major swings in the bond market.

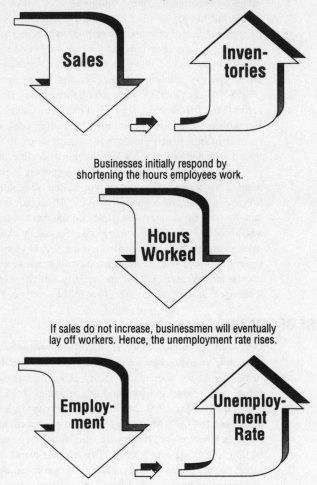

Figure 5-3 **Umemployment Rate is a Lagging Indicator of Economic Activity**

As sales decline, inventory levels begin to climb.

Sales

Inven-tories

Businesses initially respond by
shortening the hours employees work.

Hours
Worked

If sales do not increase, businessmen will eventually
lay off workers. Hence, the unemployment rate rises.

Employ-ment

Unemploy-ment
Rate

PAYROLL EMPLOYMENT IS HARD TO PREDICT

The change in payroll employment is particularly hard to
predict because we do not have a great deal of data on which
to base a forecast. Most economists look at weekly initial
unemployment claims, and/or the number of people who are

receiving unemployment insurance benefits. Others try to glean some insight from the purchasing managers' report, particularly from the employment category. However, the truth is that none of these data correlate well with payroll employment. The initial claims and benefits data seem to be more helpful in forecasting changes in the unemployment rate. The purchasing managers' index may give us some idea of what is happening to employment in the manufacturing sector, but that is about all it reveals. Unfortunately, manufacturing represents slightly less than 20% of total employment. Because we do not have much to go on, our forecast errors tend to be large. Since our projections can be far off the mark — and this report is so important — it frequently is a major market mover.

EMPLOYMENT DATA BASED ON TWO SEPARATE SURVEYS

The monthly report is derived from two surveys of employment *(Fig. 5-4)*. The labor force, household employment, and the unemployment rate are calculated from what is known as the "household survey." The payroll employment statistics, the average workweek, overtime, average hourly earnings,

 Payroll Employment and the Unemployment Rate Are Derived from Separate Surveys

Figure 5-4

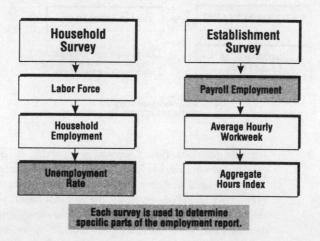

Household Survey → Labor Force → Household Employment → Unemployment Rate

Establishment Survey → Payroll Employment → Average Hourly Workweek → Aggregate Hours Index

Each survey is used to determine specific parts of the employment report.

and the aggregate hours index are derived from the "establishment survey." Both surveys are conducted by the Bureau of Labor Statistics (BLS) — a unit of the Department of Labor — for the calendar week that includes the 12th of the month. The data are generally released the first Friday of the following month.

HOUSEHOLD SURVEY — TO BE COUNTED AS "UNEMPLOYED" YOU MUST BE OUT OF WORK *AND* ACTIVELY LOOKING FOR A JOB

The household survey provides the basis for calculating the unemployment rate. Each month the BLS collects information from a sample of 59,500 households. To be included in the ranks of the unemployed, you have to satisfy two criteria: first, you have to be unemployed and, second, you have to be actively seeking employment *(Fig. 5-5)*. Basically, the BLS

Figure 5-5 Who is "Unemployed" and Who is Not

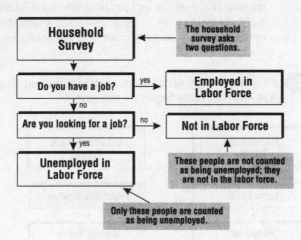

asks two questions. First, "Are you employed?" If you say yes, then you are automatically a part of the labor force, and thereby counted as being employed. If you happen to be temporarily laid off or on strike, the BLS still counts you as employed in this particular survey. If you are not employed, they then ask, "Are you looking for work?" If you say no, you are not included in the labor force and, therefore, have no impact on the calculation of the unemployment rate. If you say yes, you are officially registered as being both unemployed and a member of the labor force. This means that you now have the somewhat dubious distinction of being incorporated in the unemployment statistics for that month.

THERE ARE TWO DIFFERENT MEASURES OF THE UNEMPLOYMENT RATE

To calculate the unemployment rate, BLS will divide the number of people that are unemployed by the number of people in the labor force *(Fig. 5-6)*. Most analysts, however, refer to the *civilian* unemployment rate, which excludes the military. By definition, all members of the military have jobs — the unemployment rate amongst the armed forces is zero. Inclusion of the military essentially biases the unemployment rate slightly downward. Hence, the civilian rate is presumably more sensitive to changes in economic activity.

Figure 5-6 How the Unemployment Rate is Calculated

$$\text{Unemployment Rate} = \frac{\text{Number of People Unemployed}}{\text{Labor Force}}$$

For October 1990, we had the following:

$$5.7\% = \frac{7,073}{124,784} \text{ (thousands)}$$

ESTABLISHMENT SURVEY

ESTABLISHMENT SURVEY DATA ARE GENERALLY REGARDED AS MORE ACCURATE

Payroll employment, the average workweek, average hourly earnings, overtime, and the aggregate hours index are all calculated from the establishment survey. Once again, the data are collected from a large survey, but this time the responses come directly from businesses. For this reason, it is generally regarded as more accurate. The problem with the household survey is that, when government representatives ask questions about employment, they often get less than truthful answers for a variety of reasons. Some people may fear that the data will be reported to the immigration authorities. Others may worry that if they truthfully say they are not looking for work they may jeopardize their unemployment benefits. Employers, however, have no reason to avoid the questions and will usually give straightforward answers.

THESE TWO SURVEYS MEASURE EMPLOYMENT IN VERY DIFFERENT WAYS

One problem that occurs regularly is that these two surveys invariably produce different estimates of employment — sometimes startlingly different results — which make analysis difficult. Some of the discrepancy results from differences in coverage and definition *(Fig. 5-7)*. For example, the household surveys include self-employed workers and domestics. Because these people are not on a payroll, they obviously are not included in the establishment survey. Also, in the household survey, a person is counted only once even if he or she may have more than one job. In the establishment survey, however, a worker may be counted several times. If he or she has two jobs, and is on the payroll of two different employers,

Figure 5-7 The Two Employment Surveys Have Numerous Differences

| | Employment as Measured by: | |
	Household Survey	Establishment Survey
Wage Earners		
First Job	Yes	Yes
Second Job	No	Yes
On Strike	Yes	No
Self-Employed Workers	Yes	No
Undercounts People with Two Jobs	Yes	No
Doublecounts People with Two Jobs	No	Yes

the person is counted twice. Finally, recall that if someone is temporarily laid off or on strike, they are counted as employed in the household survey. That is not the case with payroll employment. If a person is on strike and therefore off the payroll throughout the entire survey period, he or she is not counted as employed in the establishment survey.

WHICH SURVEY SHOULD WE LOOK AT? IT IS NOT CLEAR, BUT PROBABLY BOTH

The payroll survey probably is more important because the markets react to it; but it is not entirely clear which survey is the better measure of employment. Even the experts are puzzled. As shown in *Figure 5-8*, the ratio of establishment payrolls to household workers has been rising. In fact, the payroll employment survey has recorded two million more jobs than the household survey has since the current expansion began in 1982. How can this be? This discrepancy began to appear as early as 1984, but it widened appreciably in mid-1987. An article published in the *Monthly Labor Review* in August 1989 suggests that this gap widened in large part because of multiple job holding which, of course, boosts the payroll data. In addition, the article suggests that the estab-

Figure 5-8 The Establishment to Household Employment Ratio

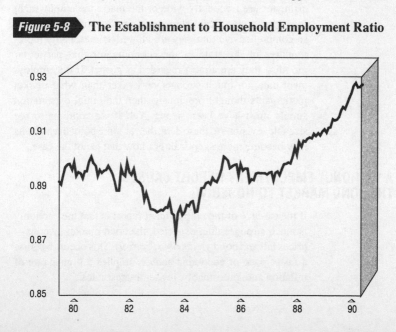

lishment of new firms plays a role in the discrepancy. Until hard data become available, the Labor Department must estimate the number of jobs originating from new firms based on historical trends. If the actual rate of job creation is not as strong as it was previously in the business cycle, the payroll data will again be overstated. Finally, the article suggests that population estimates and the difficulty of estimating the inflow of aliens into the country are factors. If the number of illegal immigrants has been growing rapidly, the household estimates will be understated. In short, there are a number of valid reasons for differences between these two surveys. But because it is not clear which survey is presenting a more accurate picture of the labor situation at the moment, it is worthwhile for you to be aware of the employment changes registered by both.

THE EMPLOYMENT REPORT HAS A MAJOR MARKET IMPACT BECAUSE IT SETS THE TONE FOR THE ENTIRE MONTH

As noted earlier, this report has the potential to be a major market mover. This occurs for two reasons. First of all, since employment data are very difficult to forecast and market estimates are frequently wide of the mark, the employment report has a significant surprise factor. Second, the data are so comprehensive that they are viewed as reasonably representative of the state of the economy for that particular month — they are almost regarded as gospel. If the employment data are much stronger or weaker than what market participants thought previously, then the initial expectation simply must have been wrong. Yet, if we continue to see sizeable revisions to these data, then at some point the markets may become more skeptical. For now that is not the case.

A "STRONG" EMPLOYMENT REPORT CAUSES THE BOND MARKET TO NOSEDIVE

If the essence of the employment report is that the economy is much stronger than expected, the bond market swoons — prices fall and bond yields rise *(Fig. 5-9)*. This occurs because a faster pace of economic activity implies a higher rate of inflation and, presumably, higher interest rates.

Figure 5-9 Market Reaction to the Employment Data

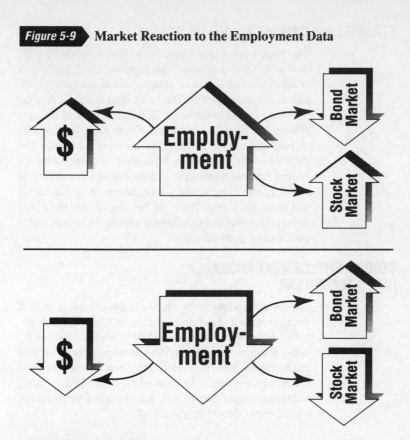

MARKET REACTION BASED UPON COMBINATION OF EMPLOYMENT, HOURS, EARNINGS, AND THE UNEMPLOYMENT RATE

This sense of whether the employment report is strong or weak depends upon several different elements, the most important of which is payroll employment. However, the markets also take into consideration the length of the workweek, factory employment, and even the unemployment rate. Furthermore, the change in average hourly earnings is viewed as an indicator of wage pressures. If wages are rising rapidly, the cost of production is also climbing — therefore the inflation rate is likely to rise. A "weak" employment report is viewed positively by the fixed-income market.

STRONG EMPLOYMENT BOLSTERS STOCKS

The stock market generally favors more economic growth than less. Thus, a "strong" employment report indicates a healthier pace of economic activity which, presumably, enhances corporate profits. The stock market should respond positively to that information. In addition, a bit of inflation probably is good for the stock market because it enables corporations to raise prices. This, too, boosts earnings. But there is a caveat to all of this. If the report is so strong that the Federal Reserve responds by raising interest rates, or if there is a sharp rise in inflationary expectations, the stock market will react adversely. Thus, the best report for the equity market is one that shows moderate growth. Too much, in this case, is not a good thing.

STRONG EMPLOYMENT PROBABLY HELPS THE DOLLAR

The dollar responds to the likely change in interest rates. If the employment report is indicative of a stronger-than-expected economy, then presumably this implies either an increase in interest rates or less of an interest rate drop-off than had been anticipated previously. If interest rates are expected to rise, then this boosts the value of the dollar. Thus, a strong employment report generally is viewed as a plus for the dollar; a weak one is viewed negatively. ✢

6

Producer Price Index

Sneak Preview of Inflation

Importance: ☆ ☆ ☆
Published by: **Bureau of Labor Statistics of the U.S. Department of Labor**

Availability: **9th – 16th of the month**
Frequency: **Monthly**
Volatility: **Moderate**

HOW THE MARKETS REACT:

Fixed-income:
PPI ⇑ ⇒ ⇓ BOND MARKET
PPI ⇓ ⇒ ⇑ BOND MARKET

Equity:
PPI ⇑ ⇒ ⇓ STOCK MARKET
PPI ⇓ ⇒ ⇑ STOCK MARKET

Dollar:
PPI ⇑ ⇒ UNCERTAIN
PPI ⇓ ⇒ UNCERTAIN

NOTEWORTHY CHARACTERISTICS:

✔ First indicator of inflation each month.

KEEPING TABS ON INFLATION IS OF UTMOST IMPORTANCE

For every investor, keeping tabs on inflation is of utmost importance. The pace of inflation, whether measured by the PPI, the CPI or one of the GNP price deflators, influences everything from Federal Reserve policy to picking the right mutual fund. But, it also matters from whence inflation comes — oil shocks, drought, labor settlements, or medical care costs *(Fig. 6-1)*. Some of these causes indicate prolonged or widespread problems, whereas others are short-lived or isolated events. One must be careful to sort out the differences. For example, sharply rising compensation levels are more serious than a poor harvest, because the latter only boosts the inflation rate *temporarily*. A drought undoubtedly causes the prices of agricultural products to rise, but once new crops are planted and harvested, price levels should decline. That is not the case with wages — they go up, but they seldom go back down.

Figure 6-1 ▶ **Inflation Can Stem from Any of Several Causes**

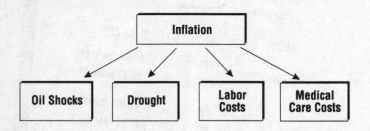

3%-4% INFLATION GENERALLY IS DEEMED ACCEPTABLE

Historically, it is safe to characterize overall inflation as tolerable or intolerable. We are quite used to price increases of 3%-4%, although many thoughtful observers would say these rates are "too high." But from a purely political viewpoint, these increases are not extreme. However, when inflation accelerates into the 6%-10% area, the ball game changes. The public demands that "something be done."

THERE ARE SEVERAL WAYS
TO COMBAT INFLATION

In the past, Washington policy makers have responded with wage and price controls, price "guidelines," or severe Federal Reserve restraint *(Fig. 6-2)*. In any case, the result is usually the same: as *Figure 6-3* demonstrates, it is no coincidence that the last two recessions quickly followed double-digit inflation rates. For this reason alone, investors must monitor and, if possible, attempt to predict broad price trends. One important source of information arrives monthly via the producer price index or PPI.

Figure 6-2 **Ways to Combat Inflation**

PPI IS THE FIRST REPORT ON INFLATION

The PPI is a measure of prices at the *producer* level and is the first inflation report to hit the "Street" each month. Since the PPI is released prior to its more famous cousin, the Consumer Price Index, some analysts simply look at "wholesale" prices to predict retail prices. But that is not a good strategy. Although *Figure 6-4* indicates a high degree of correlation over time, the two indexes are quite different. Thus, month to month, the PPI may go one way and the CPI another.

THE PPI IS AN INDEX OF COMMODITY PRICES —
NO SERVICES ARE INCLUDED

As we note elsewhere in the book, there are a variety of inflation measures, each with its own strengths and weaknesses. Regarding the PPI, it should be understood at the

Figure 6-3 ▶ **Producer Price Index**

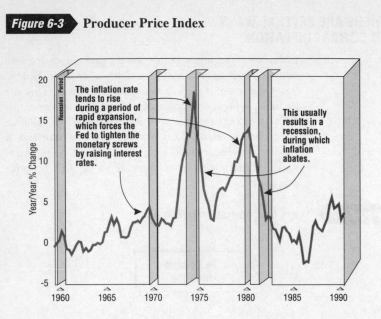

onset what is being measured — and what is not *(Fig. 6-5)*. The most important concept to remember is that the PPI is an index of *commodity* prices. In contrast, the CPI measures the prices of both commodities and *services* — housing, transportation, medical, and other services have a weighting of almost 50% in the CPI. Another difference between the CPI and PPI (for finished goods) is that the PPI measures, in part, the cost of capital goods purchased by businesses. These, of course, are not included in the CPI. Conceptually, the PPI for finished *consumer*-related goods, with a weighting of about 75%, is similar to the CPI *excluding services*. However, the PPI and CPI can behave differently owing to the differences in composition.

DATA COMPILED BY THE LABOR DEPARTMENT

How is the data put together? Labor Department economists compare prices for a multitude of items — some 3,450 commodities. Prices are sampled monthly and, in most cases, pertain to the Tuesday of the week that contains the 13th of the month. The Department analysts then weight these items in proportion to their contribution to GNP. As with the GNP

Figure 6-4 **Consumer Price Index Versus Producer Price Index**

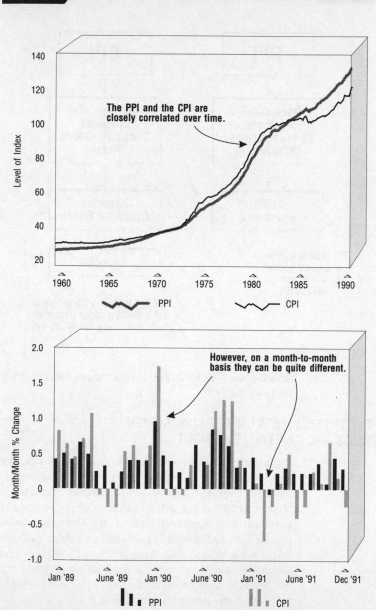

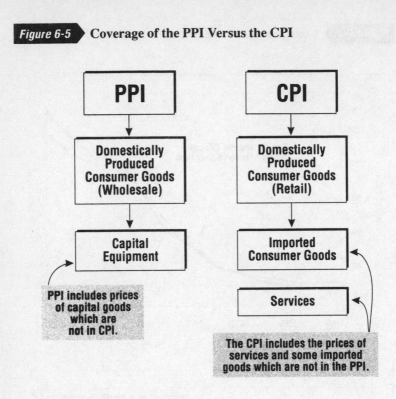

Figure 6-5 ▶ **Coverage of the PPI Versus the CPI**

deflators (see Chapter 2), the PPI is defined as equal to 100 in the base year 1982.

PPI CONTAINS DATA ON BOTH CONSUMER GOODS AND CAPITAL EQUIPMENT

When analysts and reporters refer to the PPI, they generally mean the PPI for finished goods. What are the major items in this report? *Figure 6-6* indicates that consumer-related goods account for 75% of this series. Consumer goods, principally passenger cars, represent 40% of PPI. Consumer foods provide for an additional 26%. Within consumer foods are prices for meat and fish, dairy products, and fruits and vegetables. And the energy category, largely gasoline and fuel oil, represents an additional 9% of this index. Within the capital equipment category, which accounts for the remaining 25% of the PPI, passenger cars and trucks play a

Figure 6-6 ▶ **Composition of PPI**

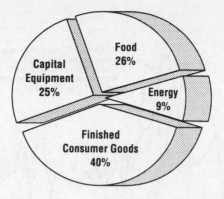

major role. You may have noticed that automobiles are included in *two* categories. This is because businesses purchase cars along with consumers. The weighting scheme of passenger vehicles in each major grouping is different, and is determined by its contribution to GNP.

MANY ECONOMISTS EXCLUDE THE VOLATILE FOOD AND ENERGY CATEGORIES

Many economists look at the PPI excluding (the often volatile) food and energy groups. This is simply another way of dissecting the data. It is a well-known fact that both food and energy prices tend to be highly volatile. Food prices, for example, may be greatly influenced by the weather and by changes in crop production. In 1980, a severe drought in many areas of the country substantially increased food prices for almost a year. For that reason, it was important to isolate the food price run-up from the rest of the PPI to get a handle on inflation's true path. Similarly, energy prices may be extremely volatile. *Figure 6-7* shows how wild these swings have been. Oil prices, for example, exploded in 1979, only to fall apart in 1986. More recently, energy prices surged again in mid-1990 with Iraq's invasion of Kuwait. Thus, when the PPI is released each month, the specialist tries to "see through" the data and determine whether the trend (or core rate) of inflation has fundamentally changed.

Figure 6-7 ▶ **PPI: Food and Energy**

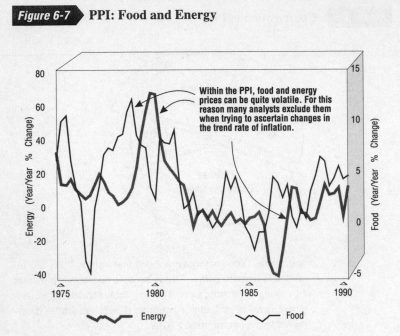

Within the PPI, food and energy prices can be quite volatile. For this reason many analysts exclude them when trying to ascertain changes in the trend rate of inflation.

——∿—— Energy   ——∿—— Food

PPI PROVIDES INFORMATION ON PRICES AT THREE STAGES OF PRODUCTION

Also note that the PPI report indicates producer prices by *stage of processing*. In fact, the data contains information on three indexes: finished goods, intermediate goods, and crude materials *(Fig. 6-8)*. As noted above, *finished goods* do not undergo any further processing. It is this category that is widely reported in the press. *Intermediate goods* are those that have undergone partial processing, but are not yet completed. *Crude materials* are just that — products entering the market for the first time, which have not been manufactured and which are not sold directly to producers. Why do we care about these other measures of inflation? We care because price changes at these earlier stages of production will frequently foreshadow movements in the PPI for finished goods.

Numerous items, representing many of the materials used by basic industry, are included in the PPI for intermediate goods: electric power, gasoline, steel, fabricated metals, and

Figure 6-8 The PPI Report Contains Price Information at Three Stages of Production

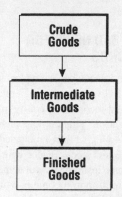

motor vehicle parts. Food plays a small role in this index. The PPI for crude materials, however, is dominated by foodstuffs. The other important elements in this index subset are energy-related — coal, natural gas, and crude petroleum.

DO NOT READ TOO MUCH INTO ANY REPORT — PPI CAN BE VOLATILE

Recall that the PPI is an *index*, with the 1982 average equal to 100. However, it is the monthly *change* in the index that is widely reported by the wire services. For example, the index rose to 108.3 in July 1988 from 107.8 in June, which represents a 0.4636 percent change. To *annualize* this rate, add a one to the number (1.004638) and raise it to the 12th power, which equals 5.7%. However, it is best not to think in these terms — the slightest variation in a month-to-month change leverages the annualized rate which occasionally results in wild looking numbers. The "professionals" generally look at the situation in a broader context and will consider a variety of approaches:

» Compare the most recent month to the prior two to three months;

» Take a look at a *moving average* of PPI releases for the past six or twelve months; or

» Determine year-over-year inflation rates.

And so forth. The point here is that investors may get burned by reading too much into an isolated report. It is better to identify a *trend* and decide whether or not a new direction is under way.

SHARP RISE IN PPI IS BAD NEWS FOR BOTH STOCKS AND BONDS

Having said that, what is a typical short-term market response *(Fig. 6-9)?* Given a PPI report — or any other inflation measure — the fixed-income and equity markets tend to move in the same direction. This marks a change from other economic releases — a higher than anticipated rise in the PPI is bearish for both bonds and stocks. Faced with higher inflation, buyers of fixed-income instruments will demand an "inflation premium" since their coupon income is worth less in real terms. The bond's principal — to be paid back at maturity — is also worth less. While some maintain that "a little inflation" is good for stocks, history shows that above a certain inflation threshold, the argument is not valid. Here again, future earnings and dividend income are both subject to the same loss of purchasing power as coupon income is — security prices will adjust downward.

THE DOLLAR'S REACTION IS LESS CLEAR

As for the dollar, the situation is tricky and, on many occasions, perverse. The dollar tends to strengthen on rising short-term interest rates. This is especially true if U.S. rates are moving higher relative to foreign rates. Ironically, if a "bad" inflation number is reported — *and if the Federal Reserve is sure to tighten* — the dollar could actually rise. On the other hand, if inflation is a problem, and for whatever reason the Federal Reserve *cannot* tighten (e.g., if the economy is weakening), then common sense does indeed prevail — a string of poor inflation reports "devalues" the dollar, causing it to fall in foreign exchange markets. ⬧

Figure 6-9 **Market Reaction to PPI**

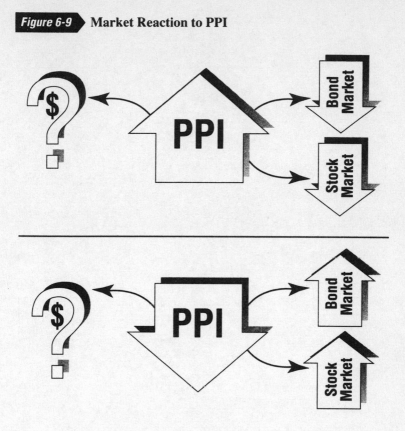

7
Retail Sales

What Is the Consumer Up To?

Importance: ☆ ☆ ☆
Published by: **Bureau of the Census of the U.S. Department of Commerce**

Availability: **11th – 14th of the month**
Frequency: **Monthly**
Volatility: **High**

HOW THE MARKETS REACT:

Fixed-income:
RETAIL SALES ⇑ ⇒ ⇓ BOND MARKET
RETAIL SALES ⇓ ⇒ ⇑ BOND MARKET

Equity:
RETAIL SALES ⇑ ⇒ ⇑ STOCK MARKET
RETAIL SALES ⇓ ⇒ ⇓ STOCK MARKET

Dollar:
RETAIL SALES ⇑ ⇒ LITTLE REACTION
RETAIL SALES ⇓ ⇒ LITTLE REACTION

NOTEWORTHY CHARACTERISTICS:

✔ Can be a major market mover.
✔ Subject to significant revisions in subsequent months.

FIRST SOLID INDICATION OF STRENGTH OR WEAKNESS IN CONSUMER SPENDING

The primary reason we are interested in retail sales is because it provides us with our first solid indication of the strength or weakness of consumer spending for a given month. What we *really* want to know is what happened to personal consumption expenditures (PCE), in real terms, for a given month. Why? Because that is the "C" (consumption) part of our familiar GNP = C + I + G + X – M equation. The reason this is so important is that consumption spending represents over one-half of GNP. Because retail sales provides us with some information about consumption, it allows us to refine our estimates of both PCE and GNP.

RETAIL SALES, EXCLUDING AUTOS, MOST IMPORTANT PART OF THIS REPORT

Probably the most important part of the retail sales report is the percentage change in sales, excluding the automobile component. The reason for this is that the Commerce Department actually uses this growth rate to estimate the non-auto, non-service portion of personal consumption expenditures. Basically, they estimate spending on services and automobiles separately, but then use the retail sales report to determine spending on everything else — which represents about 40% of the total. Thus, it is quite clear that the retail sales report supplies useful information to market participants about a significant portion of this critical GNP category.

THE REPORT HAS SEVERAL DRAWBACKS

CONTAINS DATA ON PURCHASES OF GOODS ONLY — NO SERVICES

The retail sales report, however, has a number of significant drawbacks *(Fig. 7-1)*. First of all, it only provides information about how much the consumer spends on purchases of goods. Consumption spending — which is what goes into GNP — includes purchases of both goods and services. The retail sales report tells us nothing about what the consumer may be spending on health insurance, legal fees, education, airfares, and other services.

Figure 7-1 **The Retail Sales Report Has a Few Problems**

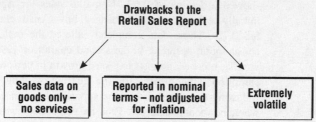

DATA REPORTED IN NOMINAL TERMS —
NOT ADJUSTED FOR INFLATION

A second problem is that retail sales are reported in *nominal* terms rather than real, i.e., adjusted for inflation. For example, retail sales in a given month could register an increase of 0.9%. Part of that rise probably reflects a larger volume of sales, but some part of the gain undoubtedly represents higher prices. Because the data that go into GNP and consumption are inflation-adjusted, it would be particularly helpful if we could split apart the 0.9% increase and say definitively that inflation-adjusted or "real" retail sales rose 0.4%, and that price increases accounted for the remaining 0.5% of the gain. But the fact of the matter is that the Census Bureau does not provide this type of breakdown. Therefore, each month economists have to examine the nominal increase and make an estimate of how much of that rise may be attributable to inflation.

DATA ARE EXTREMELY VOLATILE

Third, and probably most important, retail sales is an extremely volatile number. Not only is it hard to forecast, but it is frequently subject to massive revisions. For this reason, the preliminary retail sales data must be viewed with a considerable amount of caution. On June 13, 1990, for example, the Census Bureau reported that May retail sales declined 0.7% when the street was expecting a 0.2% increase. More important from the street's viewpoint was the fact that non-auto sales declined 0.8%. Again, analysts had been looking for a small gain. In addition, the Census Bureau reported huge downward revisions to non-auto sales in each of the two previous months. Retail sales excluding autos for March had been reported earlier as down 0.2%; after the revision, it showed a decline of 0.6%. Non-auto sales for April had initially been reported as unchanged; now Census claimed it fell 0.7%. These data completely altered the outlook for consumption spending in the second quarter of 1990. Previously, most economists expected growth in personal consumption expenditures for the quarter of about 1.5%; following this report it became apparent that consumption would be about unchanged. Thus, the PCE outlook was essentially revised downward by 1.5%. Because consumption spending represents over half of GNP, GNP forecasts for the second quarter had to be trimmed by almost 1.0% from what they had been just one day earlier.

RETAIL SALES ARE QUITE DIFFICULT TO FORECAST

The primary reason that retail sales is so difficult for analysts to forecast, is that there is not a lot of information on which to base a projection *(Fig. 7-2)*.

Figure 7-2 How to Forecast Retail Sales

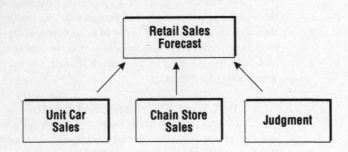

WE MUST RELY ON UNIT CAR SALES

Almost all economists track the car sales data that are released during the course of each month (see Chapter 3). However, these data tell us only the *number* of new cars that were sold each month. The monthly retail sales report reflects the *dollar value* of auto spending. In addition, the automobile component of retail sales includes sales of used cars, new and used trucks, and sales of auto parts. As a result, the unit car sales data do not provide a great deal of information about the automobile component of retail sales. And, even if one could accurately forecast this category, it only represents about 20% of the total.

AND CHAIN STORE SALES

Many economists also track the chain store sales data to evaluate the general merchandise and apparel categories, which together account for about 17% of retail sales. But the relationship between the data that are reported and what we actually see in the retail sales release is even more tenuous. Theoretically, you could simply add up the data reported for the various stores each month, divide by the seasonal factor (because the raw data are not adjusted for normal seasonal movements), and arrive at a reasonable estimate of general merchandise and apparel store sales. Yet, this does not work very well. Part of the problem may be data comparability — some chains will open new outlets, others may go out of business, and still others can merge with stores that did not report in the previous month. If the data from one month to the next are not comparable, their value as a forecasting tool is greatly diminished. A further complication is that the percentage increases that are reported by the stores are on a year-to-year basis, e.g., January of one year versus January of the previous year. But when economists analyze the retail sales data, they are interested in the change from one month to the next, e.g., December to January.

35% OF RETAIL SALES ARE ON DURABLE GOODS; 65% NONDURABLES

The retail sales data are collected monthly by the Census Bureau of the Department of Commerce from a monthly survey of retail establishments of all sizes and types throughout the country. The survey is supposed to be a statistically valid random sample that provides information on sales for a wide variety of retail establishments. For example, as shown in *Figure 7-3,* retail sales are broken down into two major categories, durables and nondurables, with the former accounting for about 35% and the latter, 65%. Durables are

Figure 7-3 Composition of Retail Sales

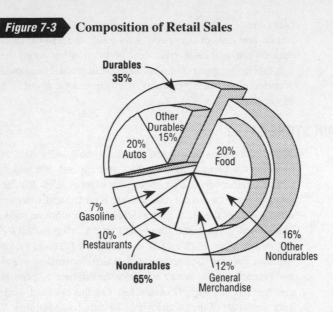

dominated — not surprisingly — by autos. Automobile and auto-related sales represent about 60% of durable goods sales. The remaining 40% are taken up by building materials, hardware, furniture, home furnishing, and household appliance sales. Nondurable goods sales are made by general merchandise (primarily department) stores, grocery stores, gas stations, apparel shops, restaurants, drug, and mail-order houses. Keep in mind that the reported data are supposed to represent sales of *merchandise* for cash or credit by establishments primarily engaged in *retail trade*. Sales of manufacturers and wholesalers are not included. Similarly, sales of service establishments are not a part of this report.

RETAIL SALES CAN BE A MAJOR MARKET MOVER — A STRONG REPORT IS NEGATIVE FOR BONDS

Because retail sales are rather difficult to forecast and the revisions are frequently large, the retail sales report has the potential to provide major surprises for the market *(Fig. 7-4)*. As a result, the market reactions can be quite pronounced. Again, the sales report released on June 13, 1990 prompted

Figure 7-4 **Market Reaction to Retail Sales**

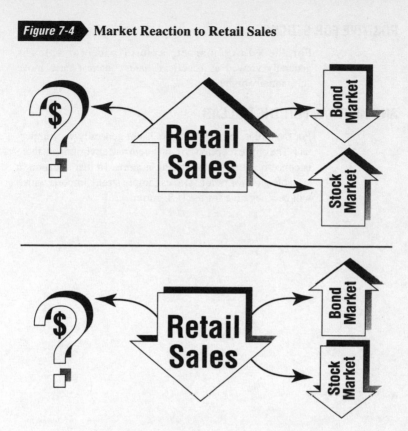

economists to lower their estimates of personal consumption spending in the second quarter by about 1.5%, and their GNP forecasts by about 1.0%. Given these revisions, market participants anticipated much less GNP growth in the second quarter, inflationary expectations were reduced, and many thought a Federal Reserve easing move was imminent. On that day, bond yields fell by 17 basis points (or .17%) to 8.45%.

Thus, a lower than expected figure for retail sales implies less GNP growth, slower inflation, and lower interest rates — suggesting that the fixed-income markets should react positively. Stronger than expected sales are viewed negatively by the fixed-income markets.

POSITIVE FOR STOCKS

For the equity market, a solid pace for sales is generally viewed as beneficial *unless* interest rates move substantially higher.

AND NEUTRAL FOR THE DOLLAR

For the dollar, retail sales news is not generally very important. The only exception is if, in the current environment, there is concern about sharply rising imports. In that situation, a sizeable gain for retail sales can imply strong imports which will be a negative for the U.S. currency. ✸

8

Industrial Production and Capacity Utilization

Goods Are Good, but What About Services?

Importance:	☆ ☆ ☆
Published by:	Board of Governors of the Federal Reserve System
Availability:	14th – 17th of the month
Frequency:	Monthly
Volatility:	Low

HOW THE MARKETS REACT:

Fixed-income:

INDUSTRIAL PROD. ⇑ ⇒ ⇓ BOND MARKET
CAPACITY UTILIZ. ⇑ ⇒ ⇓ BOND MARKET
INDUSTRIAL PROD. ⇓ ⇒ ⇑ BOND MARKET
CAPACITY UTILIZ. ⇓ ⇒ ⇑ BOND MARKET

Equity:

INDUSTRIAL PROD. ⇑ ⇒ ⇑ STOCK MARKET
CAPACITY UTILIZ. ⇑ ⇒ ⇑ STOCK MARKET
INDUSTRIAL PROD. ⇓ ⇒ ⇓ STOCK MARKET
CAPACITY UTILIZ. ⇓ ⇒ ⇓ STOCK MARKET

Dollar:

INDUSTRIAL PROD. ⇒ LITTLE REACTION
CAPACITY UTILIZ. ⇒ LITTLE REACTION

NOTEWORTHY CHARACTERISTICS:

✔ Tells us what is happening in the manufacturing sector.

✔ Easily predictable; little market impact.

INDUSTRIAL PRODUCTION REPORT TELLS US SOMETHING ABOUT GOODS PRODUCTION

ach month the Federal Reserve Board simultaneously publishes data on industrial production and capacity utilization. The index of industrial production measures the physical volume of output of the nation's factories, mines, and utilities. Taken together, these goods-producing industry groups account for about 45% of the economy *(Fig. 8-1)*. But this report tells us nothing about the pace of expansion in the service sector or in the construction industry which, combined, represent the remaining 55% of GNP. Nevertheless, we are interested in industrial production because the manufacturing sector is quite responsive to changes in economic activity. As shown in *Figure 8-2*, there is a reasonably strong correlation between production and GNP.

INFORMATION IS IN "REAL" TERMS — I.E., ADJUSTED FOR INFLATION

One advantage of the production data over many other series is that it measures changes in the *quantity* of output as opposed

Figure 8-1 **GNP: Goods Versus Services**

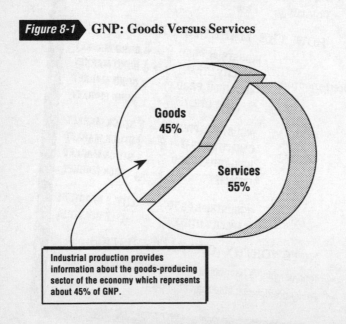

Goods
45%

Services
55%

Industrial production provides information about the goods-producing sector of the economy which represents about 45% of GNP.

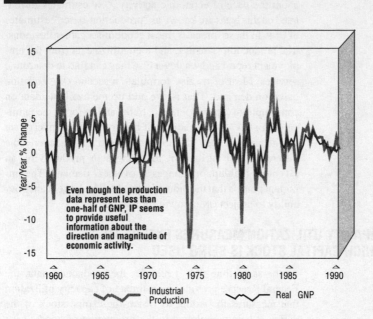

Figure 8-2 ▶ **Real GNP Versus Industrial Production**

Even though the production data represent less than one-half of GNP, IP seems to provide useful information about the direction and magnitude of economic activity.

Industrial Production   Real GNP

the *dollar volume* of that production. This corresponds closely to the concept of real GNP which attempts to measure changes in the physical output of all the goods and services produced in the economy. Many series tell us something about the dollar amount that was spent, but we cannot determine with certainty how much of that increase was attributable to a pickup in "real" spending and how much was caused by inflation. Yet, with the production data, we are seeing a "real" increase or decrease — it measures the change in the quantity of output produced. We do not have to worry about the extent to which inflation may be distorting the data.

INDUSTRIAL PRODUCTION HELPS
ECONOMISTS ESTIMATE GNP

Many economists utilize this report to achieve a more accurate GNP estimate for the quarter. After all, GNP measures the inflation-adjusted dollar value of all the goods and services produced by the United States on a quarterly basis. If you know what is happening to 45% of the economy each month, it stands to reason that this should provide strong evidence about the pace of economic activity. GNP estimates formulated on this basis are known as "production-based" estimates of GNP. In these forecasts, most economists gather the industrial production statistics, and then utilize data from the employment report and whatever else they can find to determine services. Most of us also formulate a second GNP equation based on demand. That is, we add up the available data on consumption, capital spending, trade, and so forth (the familiar C + I + G + X – M equation). If both estimates converge we are happy! If they do not, analysts try to reconcile the difference and attribute it to changes in productivity, an inventory buildup, or changes in overseas demand. The important point is that the industrial production data enhance our ability to project GNP growth for that quarter.

CAPACITY UTILIZATION MEASURES EXTENT TO WHICH CAPITAL STOCK IS BEING USED

At the same time that it releases the production data, the Federal Reserve provides an estimate of capacity utilization that measures the extent to which the capital stock of the nation is being employed in the production of goods. Like production, the utilization rate rises and falls in sync with the business cycle. As the economy lifts out of recession, production accelerates and the utilization rate rises. Just beyond the peak of the cycle, production falls off and the utilization rate declines.

HIGH UTILIZATION RATES CAN BE INFLATIONARY

The reason we monitor the capacity utilization rate is because there is a threshold beyond which any further pickup in production is inflationary. Any further demand for manufactured goods outstrips the ability of manufacturers to boost production. As demand increases relative to supply, there is a tendency for prices to rise. For the most part, the general public focuses on the overall utilization rate, and there is a common perception that when the utilization rate rises above some magic level, producer prices inevitably rise. *Figure 8-3* suggests that there *is* a relationship between utilization rates and the PPI, but the level at which prices begin to climb is

Figure 8-3 Producer Price Index Versus Capacity Utilization

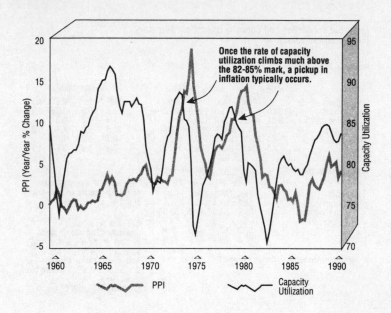

Once the rate of capacity utilization climbs much above the 82-85% mark, a pickup in inflation typically occurs.

somewhat variable — it seems to occur somewhere between 82-85%. But specialists have focused often on the utilization rate for primary-processing industries like raw steel, paper, textiles, chemicals, rubber, and plastics because late in the business cycle the combination of inventory shortages and rising demand for consumer and capital goods conspire to create price pressures in many of these industries. For this series, the so-called magic number appears to be about 85%.

INDUSTRIAL PRODUCTION IS A MEASURE OF THE PHYSICAL VOLUME OF OUTPUT

The index of industrial production measures the physical volume of output for manufacturing, mining, and utilities. The series is prepared by the Board of Governors of the Federal Reserve System and generally is available close to the 15th of the month. Since it is an index number, output is expressed as a percentage of production in some base year, currently 1987. As shown in *Figure 8-4*, this index stood at

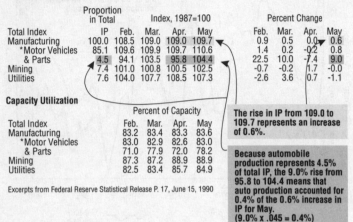

Figure 8-4 ▶ **Industrial Production and Capacity Utilization Summary**

Industrial Production and Capacity Utilization: Summary (seasonally adjusted)

Industrial Production

| | Proportion in Total | Index, 1987=100 | | | | Percent Change | | | |
	IP	Feb.	Mar.	Apr.	May	Feb.	Mar.	Apr.	May
Total Index	100.0	108.5	109.0	109.0	109.7	0.9	0.5	0.0	0.6
Manufacturing	85.1	109.6	109.9	109.7	110.6	1.4	0.2	-0.2	0.8
*Motor Vehicles & Parts	4.5	94.1	103.5	95.8	104.4	22.5	10.0	-7.4	9.0
Mining	7.4	101.0	100.8	100.5	102.5	-0.7	-0.2	1.7	-0.0
Utilities	7.6	104.0	107.7	108.5	107.3	-2.6	3.6	0.7	-1.1

Capacity Utilization

| | Percent of Capacity | | | |
	Feb.	Mar.	Apr.	May
Total Index				
Manufacturing	83.2	83.4	83.3	83.6
*Motor Vehicles	83.0	82.9	82.6	83.0
& Parts	71.0	77.9	72.0	78.2
Mining	87.3	87.2	88.9	88.9
Utilities	82.5	83.4	85.7	84.9

Excerpts from Federal Reserve Statistical Release P. 17, June 15, 1990

The rise in IP from 109.0 to 109.7 represents an increase of 0.6%.

Because automobile production represents 4.5% of total IP, the 9.0% rise from 95.8 to 104.4 means that auto production accounted for 0.4% of the 0.6% increase in IP for May.
(9.0% x .045 = 0.4%)

109.7 in May 1990, which means that production in that month was 9.7% higher than it was on average in 1987. The data are usually expressed as percent increases or declines relative to the prior month. For example, in April 1990 the index stood at 109.0. Thus, between April and May the series rose 0.6% or (109.7-109.0)/109.0.

THE FEDERAL RESERVE USES SOME HARD DATA, BUT A GREAT DEAL MUST BE ESTIMATED

To construct the index, the Board uses two types of data. In some areas of production the Federal Reserve can get a direct measure of the physical amount of goods produced. In other cases, where direct measurement is impossible, the Federal Reserve estimates output by using a combination of hours worked by production workers (from the monthly employment report) and of industrial electric power consumption. For that reason, it is not surprising that the data on employment and hours worked by manufacturing workers released by the Bureau of Labor Statistics each month are extremely helpful in forecasting the change in industrial production. Of the various economic indicators, industrial production is probably the easiest to predict.

WE CAN DETERMINE ANY PARTICULAR CATEGORY'S CONTRIBUTION TO THE TOTAL CHANGE

Once the Federal Reserve has deduced the volume of production for about 250 individual series, it multiplies each series by the weight that particular component had in the base year. It then adds up the contribution from each of these separate categories to determine the overall index. This method has the advantage of allowing us to determine the contribution stemming from any one particular category. For example, in *Figure 8-4* we can see that the index for motor vehicles and parts rose from 95.8 to 104.4 in May 1990, a gain of 9.0%. That same chart reveals that the motor vehicles category represents 4.5% of the series. Thus, one may conclude that the automobile category alone accounted for 0.4% of the overall increase of 0.6% (9.0% × .045).

CAPACITY UTILIZATION MEASURES THE PERCENT OF MAXIMUM *SUSTAINABLE* OUTPUT BEING USED

Capacity utilization is the ratio of the index of industrial production to a related index of capacity. The production measure, discussed in detail previously, is rather straightforward but the capacity part of the equation is a bit ambiguous. What is "capacity" supposed to represent? The maximum amount of output that can be generated in the event of war? The maximum amount of output that can be produced without giving rise to inflation? The Federal Reserve has decided that it does not want to measure peak output. Rather, it attempts to define a realistically sustainable maximum level of output. It defines capacity as the maximum level of production that can be obtained using a normal employee work schedule, with existing equipment, and allowing normal downtime for maintenance, repair, and cleanup. This means that two companies, with identical equipment but with different work schedules, can have different capacities. (It also means that in times of peak production, utilization rates can sometimes exceed 100.0% which, at first blush, seems impossible.)

ONCE INDUSTRIAL PRODUCTION HAS BEEN PROJECTED, CAPACITY UTILIZATION IS EASY TO ESTIMATE

Once economists have made their forecast of industrial production, by definition they also have made their projection of capacity utilization because capacity is estimated to grow at a steady pace each month. Typically, the monthly increase in capacity utilization is about 0.2% less than the rise in production.

A FASTER PACE OF PRODUCTION LEADS TO A BOND MARKET SELL-OFF

The Industrial Production report tells us something about the pace of economic activity. Presumably, a faster pace of production indicates a more rapid rate of economic activity, which leads to either increases in interest rates or smaller declines than were predicted previously. Thus, an unanticipated rise in industrial production usually prompts a sell-off in the bond market *(Fig. 8-5)*. However, economists generally have been able to deduce the change in this series far in advance of its release. As a result, the outcome is usually well-anticipated and the market reaction is small.

A STOCK MARKET RALLY

The equity markets also view a rise in production as indicative of a faster pace of economic activity which, for them, is positive. But, as is the case for bonds, production is not usually much of a market-mover.

A FASTER PACE OF PRODUCTION INCREASES THE VALUE OF THE DOLLAR

The dollar typically does not respond much to changes in production. In theory, however, a faster rate of growth in the economy leads to higher short-term interest rates. Thus, an unanticipated increase in industrial production boosts the dollar to some extent.

Figure 8-5 Market Reaction to Industrial Production

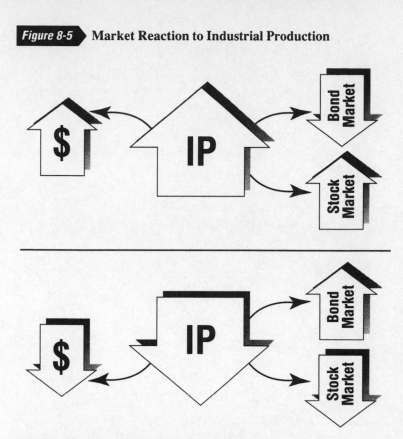

CHANGES IN UTILIZATION RATES GENERALLY ARE NOT IMPORTANT TO THE MARKETS

Changes in capacity utilization generally are not very important to the markets because they are directly related to production. If economists miss their forecast of production, they also, by definition, will be off target on their estimate of capacity utilization. The only time the utilization rate seems to be important is when it climbs to about 82%. Then market participants pay more attention and begin to worry about bottlenecks and a possible rise in inflation — bad news for both bonds and stocks. ✿

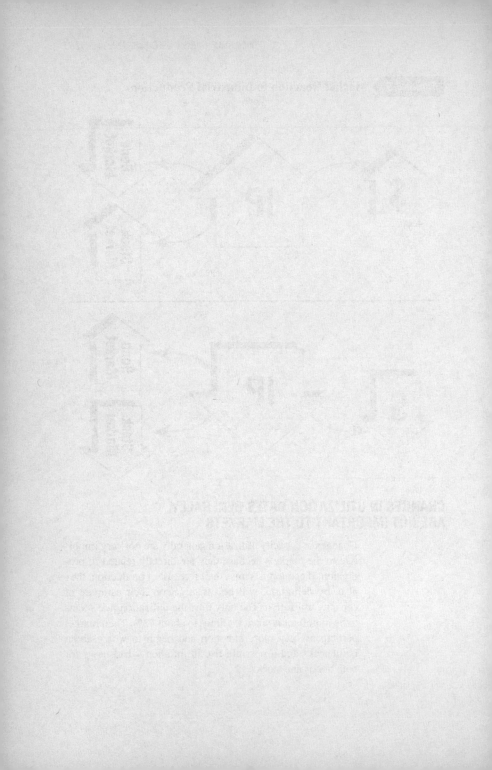

9

Housing Starts/ Building Permits

Helter Shelter

Importance:	☆☆☆
Published by:	**Bureau of the Census of the U.S. Department of Commerce**
Availability:	**16th – 20th of the month**
Frequency:	**Monthly**
Volatility:	**Moderate**

HOW THE MARKETS REACT:

Fixed-income:	HOUSING STARTS ⇑	⇒	⇓ BOND MARKET
	HOUSING STARTS ⇓	⇒	⇑ BOND MARKET
Equity:	HOUSING STARTS ⇑	⇒	⇑ STOCK MARKET
	HOUSING STARTS ⇓	⇒	⇓ STOCK MARKET
Dollar:	HOUSING STARTS ⇑	⇒	NO REACTION
	HOUSING STARTS ⇓	⇒	NO REACTION

NOTEWORTHY CHARACTERISTICS:

✔ A leading indicator of economic activity — the first indicator to turn down when the economy goes into recession; the first to rise when it rebounds.

✔ Can be quite volatile, particularly during winter months.

THE HOUSING SECTOR TENDS TO LEAD
THE REST OF THE ECONOMY

ousing starts are an extremely important indicator when forecasting the economy because most economic turnarounds in the post World War II period have been precipitated by changes in household spending habits. Invariably, these changes become apparent first in the housing and automobile sectors of the economy *(Fig. 9-1)*. This occurs partly because these types of expenditures account for such a large portion of consumer spending *(Fig. 9-2)*. It is fairly obvious that if the consumer is concerned about the outlook for the economy and the impact on his or her job six months from now, or worried about the level of interest rates and the ability to repay debts, he or she is probably going to postpone plans to buy a new house or new car as both represent "big ticket" items in the family budget.

Figure 9-1 ▶ **Housing Starts**

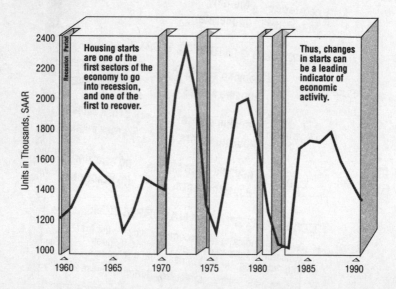

Figure 9-2 ▶ United States Household Budget

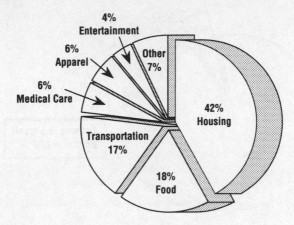

HOUSING IS A VERY IMPORTANT SECTOR
OF THE ECONOMY

Since the housing sector accounts for about 27% of investment spending and 5% of the overall U.S. economy *(Fig. 9-3),* a sustained decline in housing starts causes the economy to slow down and possibly head into recession. Likewise, a sharp rise in starts accomplishes the opposite — it boosts economic activity which could eventually pull the economy out of recession. Keep in mind that these figures only represent the direct effect of housing on the economy. It is also important to recognize that there is a multiplier effect that takes place because the demand for housing-related durables, like furniture and appliances, is tied closely to housing market activity.

CHANGES IN HOUSING ARE TRIGGERED
BY CHANGES IN MORTGAGE RATES

Changes in housing starts generally are triggered by changes in interest rates, especially mortgage rates *(Fig. 9-4).* High rates ultimately result in a decline for home sales which, in turn, produces a drop-off in starts. Conversely, low mortgage rates tend to spur both housing sales and starts.

Figure 9-3 Housing: GNP Versus Investment

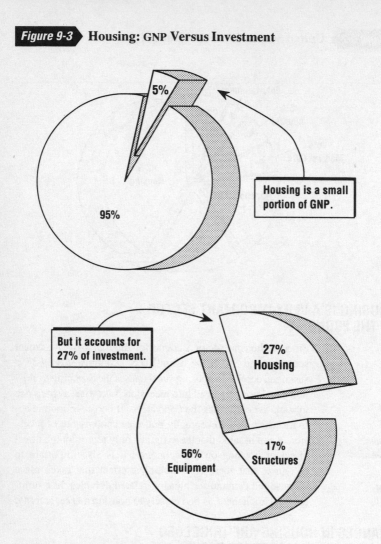

REPORT PROVIDES DATA ON BOTH SINGLE- AND MULTI-FAMILY DWELLINGS

Data on privately owned housing starts are collected by the Bureau of the Census, a unit of the Department of Commerce. Starts are divided into single-family and multi-family categories *(Fig. 9-5)*. In both cases, a housing unit is considered "started" when excavation actually begins. A single-family home counts as one start; a 100-unit apartment building

Figure 9-4 Mortgage Rates Versus New Home Sales

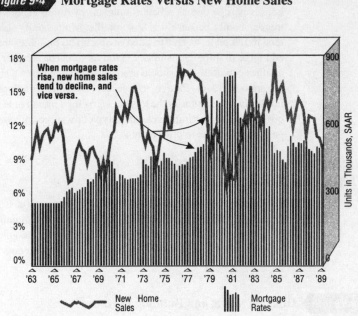

When mortgage rates rise, new home sales tend to decline, and vice versa.

New Home Sales

Mortgage Rates

Figure 9-5 New Privately Owned Housing Units Started

New Privately-Owned Housing Units Started (thousands, SAAR)

		Total	1 unit	2-4 units	5 units or more	North-east	Mid-west	South	West
1990:	April	1,216	898	53	265	124	284	469	339
	May	1,206	897	36	273	127	256	487	336
	June	1,189	889	42	258	113	241	535	300
	July	1,153	875	29	249	113	225	493	322
	August	1,142	841	31	270	118	241	440	343
	Sept.	1,135	877	36	222	105	249	453	328

The starts data are divided into single-family and multi-family categories,

as well as into four geographic areas.

counts as 100 starts. In general, construction of single-family houses is regarded as a better indicator of future economic trends, mainly because it is less volatile. Multi-family starts tend to fluctuate, as construction of apartment buildings may add large multiple units in any given month. The weather is another condition one should monitor when analyzing a single month's data. Particularly adverse weather conditions may reduce temporarily the level of starts for a month or two, but as the weather improves, starts typically surge and compensate for losses in prior months.

CHANGES IN BUILDING PERMITS LEAD STARTS BY ABOUT ONE MONTH

Building permits are released along with housing starts. Collected monthly from some 17,000 permit issuers, the number of permits issued frequently provides clues to the upcoming month's level of starts *(Fig. 9-6)*. One should expect starts to

Figure 9-6 Housing Starts and Building Permits

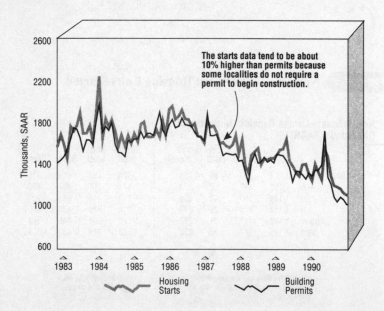

The starts data tend to be about 10% higher than permits because some localities do not require a permit to begin construction.

be about 10% higher than permits, as a general rule, simply because some localities do not require permit issuance. Since permits are such a good indicator of future economic activity, the Commerce Department includes this series in its index of leading economic indicators (see Chapter 13).

A RISE IN STARTS PROMPTS A BOND MARKET SELL-OFF

Starts and permits typically presage changes in the level of economic activity and GNP. Therefore, a larger than expected increase in either series is viewed negatively by the fixed-income market *(Fig. 9-7)*. A weaker than expected report is taken bullishly, since a soft housing sector ultimately leads to lower interest rates.

Figure 9-7 **Market Reaction to Housing Starts**

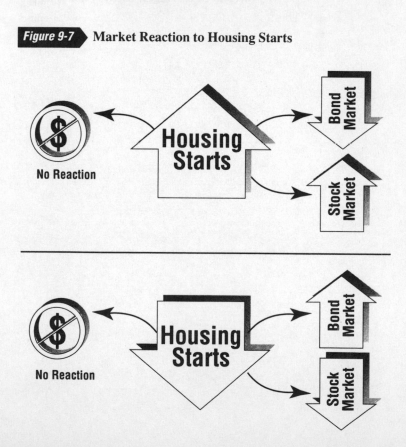

STOCKS COULD GO UP OR DOWN DEPENDING ON THE BUSINESS CYCLE

The stock market's response to housing starts and permits is usually tied to the outlook for the economy. However, the reaction may be positive or negative depending upon where we are in the business cycle. If inflation is a concern (usually late in the cycle), a lower than expected starts figure could be construed bullishly. Conversely, early in the cycle, equity players prefer strength in the housing sector, especially if interest rates are not particularly bothersome.

THE DOLLAR SHOULD NOT BE AFFECTED

The U.S. dollar is generally not affected by housing reports unless the Federal Reserve is trigger-happy to ease or tighten credit. ↕

10

Consumer Price Index

What Is Your Wallet Really Worth?

Importance:	☆☆☆
Published by:	**Bureau of Labor Statistics of the U.S. Department of Labor**
Availability:	**15th – 21st of the month**
Frequency:	**Monthly**
Volatility:	**Moderate**

HOW THE MARKETS REACT:

Fixed-income:
- CPI ⇑ ⇒ ⇓ BOND MARKET
- CPI ⇓ ⇒ ⇑ BOND MARKET

Equity:
- CPI ⇑ ⇒ ⇓ STOCK MARKET
- CPI ⇓ ⇒ ⇑ STOCK MARKET

Dollar:
- CPI ⇑ ⇒ UNCERTAIN
- CPI ⇓ ⇒ UNCERTAIN

NOTEWORTHY CHARACTERISTICS:

✔ Widely regarded as the most important inflation measure.

CPI IS THE MOST WIDELY UTILIZED MEASURE OF INFLATION

The consumer price index (CPI) is widely regarded as *the* measure of inflation although, as we will see later, it does have some drawbacks. The CPI is a measure of prices at the consumer level for a fixed basket of goods and services. Since it is an index number, it compares the level of prices to some base period. Currently, the base period is the average level of prices that existed between 1982-1984, which is set to equal 100. For example, in July 1990, the index stood at 130.5, which means that prices for that fixed basket of goods and services were 30.5% higher than they were in the base period. By comparing the level of the index at two different points in time, one can make a statement about how much prices have risen in the interim. In December 1988, the CPI was 120.7; by December of 1989, it had climbed to 126.3. Dividing the latter by the former, subtracting "1," and multiplying by 100, we learn that consumer prices rose 4.6% during 1989.

THERE ARE REALLY TWO CONSUMER PRICE INDEXES — THE CPI-U AND THE CPI-W

The CPI-U relates to all urban workers which covers about 80% of the civilian population. The CPI-W, which relates to wage earners and clerical workers, is much smaller and covers only about 40% of the population. The CPI-U is the most popular version and the one that receives all of the attention in the press. When those of us in the market talk about the CPI, we really are talking about the CPI-U. But, curiously, the CPI-W is used to adjust private sector collective bargaining agreements and payments to Social Security recipients and government/military retirees. For example, Social Security cost-of-living adjustments (COLAs), which become effective on January 1 of each year, are equal to the change in the average level of the CPI-W for the third quarter of the current year from the third quarter of the previous year. (Income tax brackets, however, are indexed to the third quarter over third quarter change in the CPI-U.)

THE LABOR DEPARTMENT CONDUCTS A PERIODIC SURVEY TO DETERMINE WHAT CONSTITUTES THE CPI

To determine what items should go into the CPI, the Bureau of Labor Statistics (BLS) conducts a survey of consumer expenditures about every 10 years. That survey estimates the number of loaves of bread purchased per month by the consumer, the number of quarts of milk consumed, and so forth. The most recent extensive survey covered the period from 1982-1984. As consumer buying patterns change over the years, the items that are included in the CPI also change. From that survey of consumer expenditures, the BLS is able to determine the appropriate weights to attach to every one of the 364 items that go into the index. Each month, the Bureau combines those individual items into seven major expenditure categories which, together with the relative importance of each, are shown in *Figure 10-1*.

Figure 10-1 ▶ **CPI Weightings**

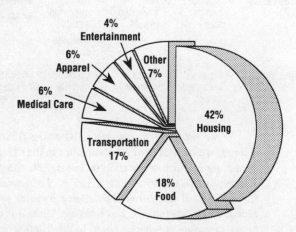

THE PRIMARY ADVANTAGE OF THE CPI IS THAT IT INCLUDES PRICES OF IMPORTED GOODS

The CPI includes imports, which is obviously very important during periods when the value of the dollar is changing rapidly. But the index also has some flaws. The biggest problem is that the coverage of the CPI is not nearly as extensive as some other measures of inflation *(Fig. 10-2)*.

Figure 10-2 Coverage of the Various Inflation Measures

	CPI	Fixed-Weight Deflator	Implicit Deflator	PPI
Domestically-Produced Consumer Goods	Yes (retail)	Yes	Yes	Yes (wholesale)
Imported Consumer Goods	Yes	No	No	No
Housing	Yes	Yes	Yes	No
Capital Equipment	No	Yes	Yes	Yes
Services	Yes	Yes	Yes	No
Biggest Drawbacks	✔ Smallest sample size	✔ No imported goods	✔ No imported goods ✔ Weights shift	✔ No services ✔ No housing
Biggest Advantages	✔ Includes imported goods	✔ Large sample size	✔ Large sample size	✔ Hints of future inflation

As we noted in the chapter on GNP, the *fixed-weight deflator,* which is the nearest competitor to the CPI in terms of importance, includes over 5,000 items. This compares to 364 items in the CPI. In addition to prices of consumer goods and services, the fixed-weight deflator includes prices of capital goods, inventories, and housing. Thus, it is a much broader measure of inflation but it, too, has deficiencies — it is strictly a domestic measure of inflation. This happens because GNP is a measure of the value of goods and services produced in the United States. The fixed-weight deflator, therefore, tells us nothing about the prices of imported goods.

Given the increasing importance of the trade sector in our economy, this is a serious drawback.

The *implicit deflator* is also important, but because the weights attached to the included goods and services are based on their relative importance to GNP, it is not really a measure of pure inflation.

Finally, the PPI is a measure of the prices that producers pay for the goods that they buy. The PPI tells us quite a bit about what is happening to commodity prices, but it tells us nothing about the housing sector or services. Since services and housing represent over one-half of the economy, the PPI is, in a sense, incomplete. Nevertheless, it provides some hints about upcoming changes in many of the goods categories included in the CPI.

All things considered, many economists regard the CPI as the most relevant measure of inflation, although every one of these four inflation indexes provides a part of the story.

ECONOMISTS CONCENTRATE ON THE CPI EXCLUDING FOOD AND ENERGY — THE CORE RATE OF INFLATION

As was the case with the PPI, economists invariably exclude the volatile food and energy components and focus on the CPI excluding food and energy, the so-called "core" rate of inflation. They do this because food prices can be quite volatile depending upon weather conditions. You may recall that there was a severe drought in 1988 which temporarily boosted food prices. However, when supplies increased later in that year, food prices fell sharply. Similarly, oil prices can, upon occasion, fluctuate wildly. If oil prices surge in one month only to plummet two months later, it makes sense to exclude their impact on the overall CPI. But economists are often accused of "ex-ing" too many items — ex food, ex energy, ex tobacco, ex autos — and perhaps some of that criticism is valid. But the reason we exclude certain items is because economists want to determine changes in the *trend* rate of inflation and do not want to be distracted by aberrations. If oil prices rise and it seems likely to be a temporary phenomenon, we rightfully should look at the CPI excluding the impact of the higher oil prices. But if oil prices rise and remain high for three to six months, that is a different story. In that situation, we should not be so quick to delete the effect of the oil price run-up.

Figure 10-3 Market Reaction to CPI

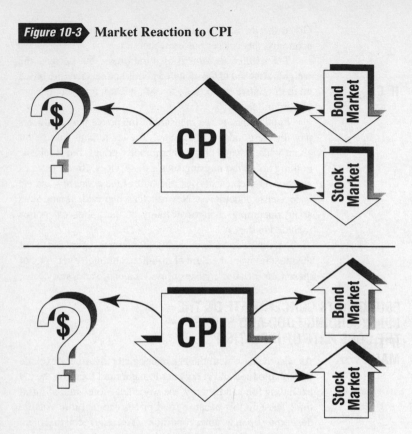

CPI INCLUDES PRICES FOR A BROAD RANGE OF CONSUMER-RELATED GOODS AND SERVICES

The consumer price index is released monthly by the Bureau of Labor Statistics of the Department of Labor. It reflects prices of food, clothing, shelter, fuels, transportation fares, charges for doctors' and dentists' services, drugs, and all sorts of other goods and services that people buy for day-to-day living. Prices are collected in 85 cities across the country on 364 different products from 18,000 tenants, 18,000 housing units, and 24,000 establishments of all kinds. The data are then weighted by their relative degree of importance and combined into the seven broad categories that were shown earlier. The CPI is released between the 15th and 21st of the month.

IF CPI RISES, THE BOND MARKET WILL FALL

The markets respond to the CPI exactly the same way they react to the PPI *(Fig. 10-3)*. A higher than expected figure is bearish for both stocks and bonds, while lower than anticipated gains are bullish. A pickup in inflation implies higher bond yields, which prompts bond price declines. Keep in mind that the reaction in the fixed-income market is tied more closely to the CPI *excluding* the frequently volatile food and energy components, because that series is believed to be a better approximation of the underlying rate of inflation. Analysts are also somewhat forgiving of a one month blip. They are not going to become too excited until they see higher than expected data for two or three consecutive months, because it takes that much time to determine whether the trend rate of inflation has changed.

IF THE CPI RISES, THE STOCK MARKET WILL FALL

A higher than expected inflation rate is also likely to trigger a stock market decline. Remember, stock prices reflect the value of a stream of future earnings. To the extent that inflation accelerates, those future earnings are clearly worth less.

THE DOLLAR'S REACTION IS LESS CLEAR

The impact on the dollar is less clear. In some theoretical sense, higher inflation should be viewed negatively by overseas investors because the return on their dollar-denominated investments will be eroded by inflation. And, in fact, a higher than anticipated rate of inflation can sometimes be dollar bearish. But, if foreign investors believe that the Federal Reserve will tighten credit and push short-term interest rates in the United States higher relative to those in other countries, the dollar can actually strengthen. This may seem a little perverse, but it has happened on a number of occasions. ✦

11

Durable Goods Orders

The Prince of Volatility

Importance:	☆ ☆
Published by:	**Bureau of the Census of the U.S. Department of Commerce**
Availability:	**22nd – 28th of the month**
Frequency:	**Monthly**
Volatility:	**Very High**

HOW THE MARKETS REACT:

Fixed-income:

DURABLE GOODS ORDERS ⇑ ⇒ ⇓ BOND MARKET

DURABLE GOODS ORDERS ⇓ ⇒ ⇑ BOND MARKET

Equity:

DURABLE GOODS ORDERS ⇑ ⇒ ⇑ STOCK MARKET

DURABLE GOODS ORDERS ⇓ ⇒ ⇓ STOCK MARKET

Dollar:

DURABLE GOODS ORDERS ⇑ ⇒ NO REACTION

DURABLE GOODS ORDERS ⇓ ⇒ NO REACTION

NOTEWORTHY CHARACTERISTICS:

✔ Extremely volatile!

ORDERS ARE A LEADING INDICATOR OF MANUFACTURING SECTOR ACTIVITY

urable goods orders have the *potential* to provide market participants with much information. Orders are believed generally to be a harbinger of activity in the manufacturing sector because a manufacturer must have an order before contemplating a step-up in production. Conversely, a drop-off in orders eventually causes production to be scaled back; otherwise the manufacturer accumulates inventories which must be financed. It should be noted that three of the 11 components of the Commerce Department's index of leading indicators represent various types of orders — new orders for consumer goods, plant and equipment orders, and the change in the backlog of orders for durable goods industries. Clearly, orders are important in anticipating changes in production; they tend to decline eight to 12 months ahead of a cyclical downturn, and begin to rise about one month ahead of the trough of a recession.

THE ORDERS DATA ARE EXTREMELY VOLATILE

Unfortunately, this series has two major drawbacks. The first problem with the orders data is that they are *extremely* volatile *(Fig. 11-1)*. There is no question that these are the most volatile of all the indicators described in this book. In the first six months of 1990, for example, the average monthly change (without regard to sign) was 5.2%, and those changes ranged in size from 2.4% to 10.5%. Durable goods orders are quite volatile because they include civilian aircraft and defense orders. If Boeing lands a big order for one of its jumbo jets, the civilian aircraft category can change by $3-4 billion. Given that the current level of durable goods orders is only $125 billion, fluctuation in the civilian aircraft category alone can easily give rise to changes of 3%. Defense orders can do the same thing — toss in an order for a B-1 bomber or an aircraft carrier, and we will see surges in the defense category as well.

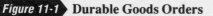

Figure 11-1 ▶ Durable Goods Orders

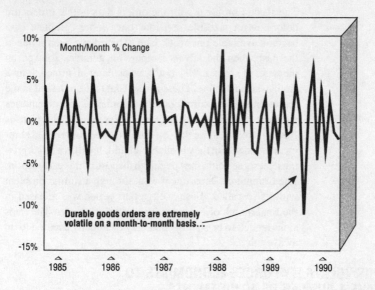

Month/Month % Change

**Durable goods orders are extremely
volatile on a month-to-month basis...**

1985   1986   1987   1988   1989   1990

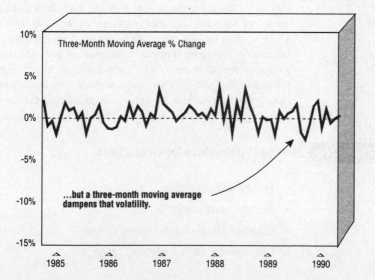

Three-Month Moving Average % Change

**...but a three-month moving average
dampens that volatility.**

1985   1986   1987   1988   1989   1990

THEY ARE NOTORIOUS FOR SIZEABLE REVISIONS

The second problem with the orders data is that orders are notorious for sizeable revisions once more complete data become available one week later. There have been times in the past when the advance report on durables showed an increase of, say, 2.0%, but a week later it turned into a similar-sized decline. These revised data are contained in the report on manufacturing orders, shipments, and inventories which is discussed in Chapter 16. Essentially, the Census Bureau releases these data on durable goods orders and shipments sooner than they probably should. It will not be surprising if, at some point, they decide to dispose of this early report. The Commerce Department went through a similar problem with its so-called "flash" GNP report which was released in the final month of a quarter for that same quarter. The revisions tended to be so large that they eventually decided to do away with it.

THIS VOLATILITY FORCES ECONOMISTS TO MAKE A NUMBER OF ADJUSTMENTS

Any series that is extremely volatile forces analysts to make a number of adjustments in order to interpret the data *(Fig. 11-2)*. The first thing they do when this figure is released is look at the data excluding the transportation category, knowing that swings in aircraft orders can be overwhelming. Analysts do the same thing with defense orders because they too can be subject to wild gyrations. By examining durable goods orders excluding transportation and excluding defense, specialists

Figure 11-2 How to Use the Durable Goods Data

» Exclude defense orders.

» Exclude transportation orders.

» Calculate a three-month moving average.

» Calculate year-to-year percent change.

get a sense for whether the monthly change is attributable to one of the extremely volatile components. If it is, they tend to dismiss its significance. If it is not, the change is probably more meaningful. Finally, analysts look at a three-month moving average, or the year-over-year percentage change, in an attempt to smooth the data and more readily determine changes in trend growth.

DURABLES ARE DIFFICULT TO FORECAST

The final point that should be made about the durable goods report is that it is particularly difficult to forecast. Indeed, many economists simply do not bother because there is very little data on which to base a forecast. The automobile production data can help us get a handle on automobile orders and shipments. And some analysts will track aircraft orders that are reported in the paper. But, unfortunately, there is little correlation between when an order is reported in the paper and when that order eventually shows up on the company's books and when it is included in the Census Bureau's data. The most we can do for many of these categories is look at the change in the prior month. If it surged in the previous month, we probably anticipate an offsetting decline in the current month and vice versa. This approach is not very sophisticated, but it appears to be all we can do when forecasting durables.

THIS REPORT ALSO CONTAINS DATA ON SHIPMENTS OF DURABLES

In addition to the data on durable goods *orders*, this report provides information on durable goods *shipments*. For purposes of this report, the term "shipments" and "sales" are basically synonymous. Since manufacturing and trade sales are generally a coincident indicator of the economy, these sales are useful in confirming the peak or trough of a business cycle. To the extent that factory sales represent about 45% of total business sales, and shipments of durables account for the volatility in the factory portion, these data help us get an early indication of when the economy reaches a turning point.

NON-DEFENSE CAPITAL GOODS CATEGORY PROVIDES INFORMATION ABOUT CAPITAL SPENDING PATTERNS

In particular, one should pay some attention to the shipments and orders of *non-defense capital goods* — these two series provide some indication of current and future capital spending by businesses. Specifically, there is a reasonable correlation between shipments of non-defense capital goods and the producers' durable equipment category of GNP. This is an important part of the investment component, the "I" part of the familiar GNP = C + I + G + X − M equation. Equipment spending accounts for nearly 10% of GNP, and about 55% of fixed investment. Thus, it is worth paying attention to the data on the shipments of non-defense capital goods to get an idea about what is happening to equipment spending in the current quarter, and to the comparable orders data to determine what is likely to occur in the months ahead.

THE BACKLOG OF ORDERS IS ALSO IMPORTANT

To some extent, the backlog measures the stack of orders on a manager's desk. Each month new orders are added to the pile. Those orders that have been filled and shipped during the course of the previous month are removed. If this pile of orders (or backlog) is growing, it makes sense that, at some point, the company will step up its pace of production.

THE CENSUS BUREAU CONDUCTS AN EXTENSIVE SURVEY TO COLLECT DATA

The data on durable goods orders, shipments, and the order backlog are compiled by the Census Bureau of the Department of Commerce from a monthly survey of approximately 5,000 manufacturers. These sample data are used to estimate a universe of some 70,000 establishments. Thus, the Census Bureau is sampling less than 10% of the existing manufacturing firms. The reported data are supposed to represent firm orders for immediate or future delivery. These orders must be legally binding — supported by a signed contract, a letter of intent, or some similar document. Options to place additional orders at some future date are *not* included. In the aircraft industry, for example, an airline could place an order to purchase 10 aircraft for delivery over the next five years, and take an option to purchase 10 additional aircraft at some point in the future. Those additional aircraft would not be included in the durable goods report until a firm order is actually submitted. The shipments data represent the sum total of sales for that month whether for domestic use or for export.

SINCE DURABLES ARE HARD TO PREDICT, SURPRISES ARE FREQUENT

Because this series is both very volatile and difficult to forecast, street projections are frequently wide of the mark. Thus, there is much room for shifts in the general perception of what is happening in the manufacturing sector. In the past, this series rarely generated much market excitement; but, more recently, there have been several occasions when the durable goods report was a market-mover.

IF DURABLES SURGE, THE BOND MARKET WILL DECLINE

If the fixed-income market is surprised by a particularly strong durable goods report, i.e., a much larger than expected increase for a particular month (perhaps in conjunction with an upward revision), the fixed-income markets react negatively *(Fig. 11-3)*. Such a report indicates more strength in the manufacturing sector and, therefore, more rapid GNP growth. If the economy is expanding more rapidly than anticipated, the markets worry about a pickup in the rate of inflation. If all of this transpires, the odds are that interest rates will rise. Naturally, the prices of fixed-income securities will decline.

STOCKS COULD GO UP OR DOWN DEPENDING ON THE BUSINESS CYCLE

The reaction in the equity market is always tough to gauge. In general, a larger than expected rise in durables is greeted favorably. When orders rise, presumably profits are enhanced, which is a plus. But there is a caveat. If the bond market sells off sharply owing to fears of higher interest rates, then the equity markets also decline — higher interest rates are always unwelcome in the equity market.

 **Market Reaction to Durables**

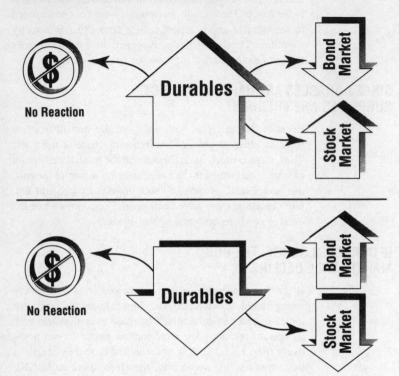

THE DOLLAR SELDOM REACTS TO THIS REPORT

In theory, a faster pace of economic activity is good for the dollar. Yet, in practice, this report is ignored in the foreign exchange market. ✸

12

Personal Income and Consumption Expenditures

You Must Have It to Spend It!

Importance:	☆ ☆ ☆
Published by:	Bureau of Economic Analysis of the U.S. Department of Commerce
Availability:	22nd – 31st of the month
Frequency:	Monthly
Volatility:	Moderate

HOW THE MARKETS REACT:

Fixed-income:	INCOME ⇑ ⇒ ⇓	BOND MARKET
	CONSUMPTION ⇑ ⇒ ⇓	BOND MARKET
	INCOME ⇓ ⇒ ⇑	BOND MARKET
	CONSUMPTION ⇓ ⇒ ⇑	BOND MARKET
Equity:	INCOME ⇑ ⇒ ⇑	STOCK MARKET
	CONSUMPTION ⇑ ⇒ ⇑	STOCK MARKET
	INCOME ⇓ ⇒ ⇓	STOCK MARKET
	CONSUMPTION ⇓ ⇒ ⇓	STOCK MARKET
Dollar:	INCOME ⇑ ⇒ ⇑	DOLLAR
	CONSUMPTION ⇑ ⇒ ⇑	DOLLAR
	INCOME ⇓ ⇒ ⇓	DOLLAR
	CONSUMPTION ⇓ ⇒ ⇓	DOLLAR

NOTEWORTHY CHARACTERISTICS:

✓ Consumption is important because it represents over one-half of GNP.

PERSONAL CONSUMPTION EXPENDITURES
REPRESENT OVER ONE-HALF OF GNP

robably the most important part of this report is the information on personal consumption expenditures (PCE) because this is by far the largest component of GNP; it represents over one-half of the total *(Fig. 12-1)*. Consumption expenditures represent the market value of all goods and services purchased by individuals. Each month we receive additional information on consumption spending which allows us to refine our GNP estimates. It is clearly not the *only* item factored into GNP, and occasionally, errors in our forecasts of trade, inventories, or government spending throw our GNP estimates off target. However, if we know what happens to more than one-half of the pie, there is no doubt that we have a few strong hints about what will happen to GNP growth for that quarter!

INCOME PROVIDES THE FUEL FOR
FURTHER SPENDING

Personal income represents the compensation that individuals receive from all sources *(Fig. 12-2)*. That includes wages and salaries, proprietors' income, income from rents, dividends and interest, and transfer payments, such as Social Security, unemployment, and welfare benefits. We are interested in income because it provides the fuel for further spending. If we do not have it, we eventually are forced to cut back. We can always borrow money, allowing us to spend for a while longer. But by doing so, we increase our monthly payments because we eventually have to pay back the loan. That means that we have just that much less to spend on other things. Pay me now, or pay me later!

A related item that is not known until approximately a week later is "real" income, or income after adjustment for inflation. If personal income is expanding, but the increase merely reflects a rise in inflation, then the consumer's welfare or "real" purchasing power has not changed. These two measures of income, nominal and real, are considered to be good barometers of the current strength of the economy.

Figure 12-1 Composition of GNP: Consumption

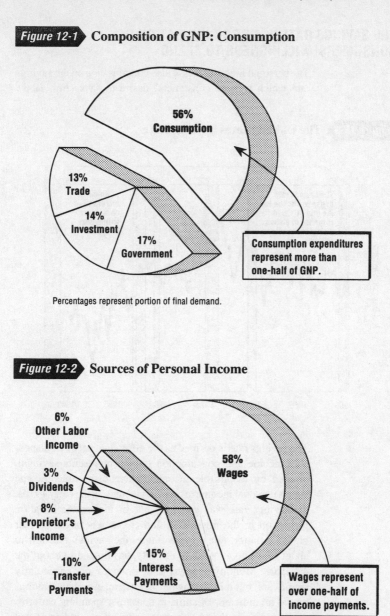

56%
Consumption

13%
Trade

14%
Investment

17%
Government

Consumption expenditures
represent more than
one-half of GNP.

Percentages represent portion of final demand.

Figure 12-2 Sources of Personal Income

6%
Other Labor
Income

3%
Dividends

8%
Proprietor's
Income

10%
Transfer
Payments

15%
Interest
Payments

58%
Wages

Wages represent
over one-half of
income payments.

THE SAVINGS RATE IS A GOOD INDICATION OF CONSUMERS' WILLINGNESS TO SPEND

The personal income release also contains data on the savings rate which reflects consumers' desire to save *(Fig. 12-3).*

Figure 12-3 ▶ **The United States Savings Rate**

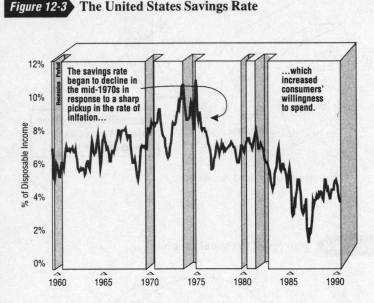

The savings rate is defined as the difference between disposable income and consumption (which represents savings), divided by disposable income (where disposable income equals personal income less tax payments). In the early 1970s, the savings rate was generally 8% or higher. As inflation picked up in the mid-1970s and consumers began to fear higher inflation rates in the future, the savings rate fell to about 6%. This rate, more recently, has dipped to about the 4% mark. Monthly changes in this rate are not particularly significant, but it is worthwhile to keep an eye on the savings rate as an indicator of shifts in consumer spending patterns. A sharp drop in the savings rate, for example, indicates that the consumer is dipping into savings to finance purchases. This is not a sustainable situation, and one should expect to see slower consumption and GNP growth in the months ahead.

INCOME ESTIMATES RELY ON DATA FROM A WIDE VARIETY OF SOURCES

The income and consumption data are prepared monthly by the Commerce Department's Bureau of Economic Analysis. Given the many different types of income, there is a wide variety of source data. For example, wage estimates are prepared primarily from the payroll employment data that is submitted by the Bureau of Labor Statistics. Data on transfer payments come from information collected by the Social Security Administration, the Veterans Administration, and the monthly statement of receipts and outlays published by the Treasury Department. Dividend income is estimated from a sample of corporate dividend payments. Interest income is derived by applying interest rates to household asset data that is collected by the Federal Reserve Board. You get the idea.

THE CONSUMPTION DATA RELY HEAVILY ON THE RETAIL SALES REPORT AND ON CAR SALES

Similarly, the monthly estimates of consumption expenditures involve data collection from many different sources. As we will see, the Commerce Department relies heavily upon trends shown in the Census Bureau's retail sales report. In addition, the Commerce Department uses the unit car sales data that are reported by each of the manufacturers. They also have some *price* data for cars, gasoline, and tobacco because prices of these items tend to be quite volatile. After all, if the price of a commodity rises sharply, the dollar amount spent also increases. It should be noted that the personal consumption data are presented in both nominal and "real" or inflation-adjusted terms. This latter series *is* the consumption portion of the GNP estimate. Simply average the figures for the three months of the quarter, and you will have the PCE component of the gross national product.

Since PCE is such an important part of GNP, it is important for investors to understand how economists formulate their forecast *(Fig. 12-4)*. The first information we receive about the pace of consumer spending for any given month stems from the data on car sales. However, these are unit data. That means we know the *number* of cars sold during the course of the month. Yet, what we really want to know is the *dollar value* of those sales. Thus, the car sales data are not perfect,

Figure 12-4 How to Forecast Consumption

Consumption Component	Source Data	Percent of Total
Automobiles	Unit car sales	6%
Other Durables	Retail sales	7%
Nondurables	Retail sales	33%
Services	None – rely on trends	54%

but they help us forecast about 6% of the PCE figure for any given month. The next tidbit of information arrives via the retail sales report, which suggests the extent of consumer spending on *goods* during the course of the month — cars, as well as food, clothing, gasoline, and furniture. In fact, the Commerce Department bases their estimate of consumer spending on goods (except for autos) on this report. With these data in hand, we now have some idea of what is happening to another 40% of consumer spending. We still have to estimate expenditures on services which represent the remaining 54% of the series. Fortunately, spending on services tends to be relatively stable and somewhat easier to predict.

These income and consumption data are compiled, edited, and eventually released one day after the publication of the GNP report — which generally appears in the third week of the month.

STRONG GAINS IN INCOME AND CONSUMPTION PRODUCE A BOND MARKET SELL-OFF

Gains in personal income indicate that the economy is growing, and increases in personal consumption expenditures show that the consumer is spending. Therefore, larger than expected gains in either personal income or consumption is viewed negatively by the fixed-income markets *(Fig. 12-5)*. These markets begin to fear that the Federal Reserve will tighten monetary policy by increasing interest rates. On the other hand, sluggish income growth or a reduced pace of spending is greeted favorably.

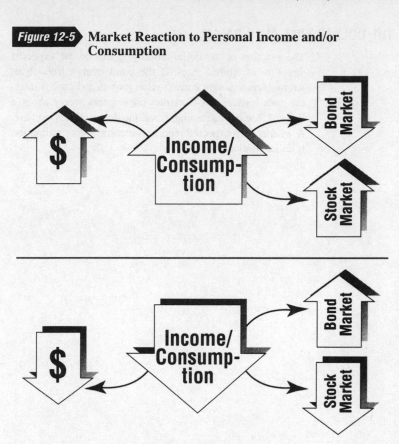

Figure 12-5 Market Reaction to Personal Income and/or Consumption

THE STOCK MARKET WILL USUALLY RALLY

For the stock market, strong income growth is generally a plus because a rapidly expanding economy usually is associated with profit growth. But, as is frequently the case with the equity markets, there is a major caveat. If the robust pace of economic activity causes market participants to believe that the Federal Reserve is going to boost interest rates, then there truly can be too much of a good thing — growth. In such a situation, the stock market will decline.

THE DOLLAR WILL ALSO RALLY

The reaction of the dollar usually is tied to the expected direction of interest rates. If the bond market frets about strong income and/or consumption growth and pushes interest rates higher, and if market participants worry about a Federal Reserve tightening move, the dollar climbs in value. A weaker than expected report on income and consumption is dollar bearish. ⬇

13

The Index of Leading Economic Indicators

An Early Warning System

Importance: ☆ ☆ ☆

Published by: **Bureau of Economic Analysis of the U.S. Department of Commerce**

Availability: **Last business day of the month**

Frequency: **Monthly**

Volatility: **Low**

HOW THE MARKETS REACT:

Fixed-income:
LEI ⇑ ⇒ ⇓ BOND MARKET
LEI ⇓ ⇒ ⇑ BOND MARKET

Equity:
LEI ⇑ ⇒ ⇑ STOCK MARKET
LEI ⇓ ⇒ ⇓ STOCK MARKET

Dollar:
LEI ⇑ ⇒ ⇑ DOLLAR
LEI ⇓ ⇒ ⇓ DOLLAR

NOTEWORTHY CHARACTERISTICS:

✔ Tells us when the economy is about to change direction.

THE INDEX OF LEADING ECONOMIC INDICATORS IS DESIGNED TO PREDICT FUTURE ECONOMIC ACTIVITY

The index of leading economic indicators (LEI), a composite of several different indicators, is designed to predict future aggregate economic activity. Historically, the LEI reaches peaks and troughs earlier than the underlying turns in the economy and therefore is an important tool for forecasting and planning *(Fig. 13-1)*. The index is composed of 11 series, all of which have varying lead times at cyclical tops and bottoms. As a rule of thumb, turning points in the economy are signaled by three consecutive monthly LEI changes in the same direction. For example, consecutive readings of -0.5%, -1.1% and -0.7% would signal a possible recession. However, even though a recession has always been preceded by three straight LEI declines, the converse is not true — since 1952, the LEI has "predicted" ten recessions, but only seven actually occurred. In other words, pronounced weakness in the index is a necessary, but not a sufficient, condition for an economic downturn.

Figure 13-1 ▶ **Index of Leading Economic Indicators**

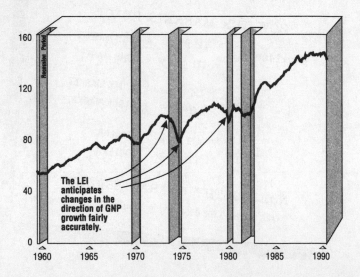

The LEI anticipates changes in the direction of GNP growth fairly accurately.

Figure 13-1 demonstrates the historical usefulness of the LEI. While the forecasting record is fairly good, it should be noted that the LEI has performed better at business cycle peaks than troughs. On average, the index has turned down ten months ahead of economic tops, although with high variability. The index seems to give less notice regarding cyclical bottoms. On average, the LEI turns up only two months ahead of these economic upswings.

EACH COMPONENT IS A LEADING INDICATOR

The LEI's individual components were chosen because of their economic significance, statistical adequacy, consistency of timing at cycle peaks and troughs, conformity to expansions and contractions, smoothness, and prompt availability *(Fig. 13-2)*. These components are weighted equally to provide a net contribution to the composite index. The specific leading indicators — selected from various sectors of the economy — include the following: the average workweek, weekly jobless claims, new orders for consumer goods, vendor performance, contracts and orders for new plant and equipment, building permits, changes in unfilled durable goods orders, sensitive materials prices, stock prices, money supply, and consumer expectations.

Figure 13-2 **Components of the Index of Leading Indicators**

1. Average workweek — manufacturing
2. Initial unemployment claims
3. New orders for consumer goods
4. Vendor performance
5. Plant and equipment orders
6. Building permits
7. Change in unfilled orders — durables
8. Sensitive material prices
9. Stock prices, S&P 500
10. Real M2
11. Index of consumer expectations

THE TOTAL INDEX PERFORMS BETTER
THAN ANY OF ITS PARTS

How do the individual components relate to the overall economy? The average workweek and jobless claims provide insight into labor market conditions. Employers frequently increase (or decrease) hours worked before hiring (or dismissing) personnel. Jobless claims indicate the amount of slack in the labor market. Consumer goods orders provide clues about future consumer spending. Vendor performance reflects the percentage of companies reporting slower deliveries, which is often a sign of bottlenecks and shortages associated with a strong economy. Unfilled durable goods orders and sensitive materials prices also offer hints regarding economic strength or weakness. Contracts for new plant and equipment reflect business investment spending plans and, by extension, business views on economic conditions. Building permits lead residential construction activity, a highly cyclical sector that has ramifications for other "big ticket" spending. Stock prices, as measured by the S&P 500, reflect consensus expectations about future earnings and overall business conditions. Changes in the money supply (M2) measure banking system liquidity, with higher liquidity associated with increased economic activity. Finally, consumer expectations, monitored by the University of Michigan's Survey of Consumer Sentiment, provide insight into consumer spending plans. Because these 11 series cover so many different sectors of the economy, they perform better as a group than any isolated series.

A VARIETY OF GOVERNMENT AGENCIES AND
PRIVATE SOURCES PROVIDE THE BASIC DATA

The LEI is compiled by the Bureau of Economic Analysis (BEA) of the Department of Commerce, using data from a variety of private sources and government agencies. A partial source list includes the departments of Commerce, Labor, Treasury, Defense, the Federal Reserve, NAPM, the Conference Board, and the National Bureau of Economic Research. The BEA releases the index on the last business day of the month, based on the prior month's information. At the time of publication, all 11 LEI components are available to the BEA.

Of these, nine are known in advance and the remaining two can be estimated fairly accurately. As a result, the index usually is forecasted with an error of less than 0.2%.

THE COMMERCE DEPARTMENT PUBLISHES TWO OTHER INDEXES OF ECONOMIC ACTIVITY

COINCIDENT INDICATORS

The Bureau of Economic Analysis also publishes an index of coincident indicators, designed to turn up or down "coincident" with changes in the economy. Thus, a rise or fall in this index suggests economic expansion or contraction in a given month. The index consists of four components:

» Employees on nonagricultural payrolls;
» Personal income less transfer payments;
» Index of industrial production; and
» Business sales.

LAGGING INDICATORS

The Bureau releases an index of lagging indicators that turn up or down four to nine months *after* the economy begins to emerge from or enter into a recession. Essentially, this index is used to confirm whether or not a turning point has occurred. This index has six components:

» Average duration of unemployment;
» Ratio of business inventories to sales;
» Index of unit labor costs for manufacturing;
» Average prime rate charged by banks;
» Commercial and industrial loans; and
» Ratio of consumer installment debt to personal income.

THE RATIO OF COINCIDENT TO LAGGING INDICATORS MAY BE THE BEST LEADING INDICATOR OF ALL

Separately, the coincident and lagging indicators series are of little market significance. But the *ratio* of coincident to lagging indicators provides clues to economic turnarounds *sooner* than the leading indicators series itself *(Fig. 13-3)*. Why is this so? The answer lies in the business cycle: in the early stages of an economic upswing, coincident indicators rise, while the lagging series — which depict the economy

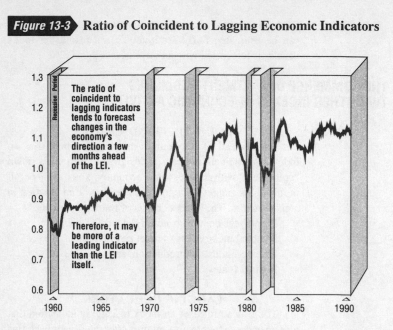

Figure 13-3 Ratio of Coincident to Lagging Economic Indicators

several months earlier — remains essentially unchanged. Thus, the ratio (coincident/lagging) is rising. Near the peak of an expansion, the rate of increase in the coincident index is less than the rate of increase in the lagging series. Consequently, the ratio begins to fall — possibly signaling a major turning point. Near the trough of a recession, the rate of decline in the coincident series is smaller than the rate of decline in the lagging index — the ratio rises. As *Figure 13-3* suggests, this ratio tends to signal economic turnarounds about two months ahead of the LEI itself.

THE MARKETS SELDOM REACT TO THIS REPORT

A leading index report seldom shocks the markets, despite its usefulness as a forecasting tool *(Fig. 13-4)*. Since most of the 11 components are known through prior releases, forecasts of the LEI's performance are generally accurate. Even so, surprises occasionally occur. The markets usually respond to surprises as they do toward any other macroeconomic indica-

Figure 13-4 **Market Reaction to the Index of Leading Indicators**

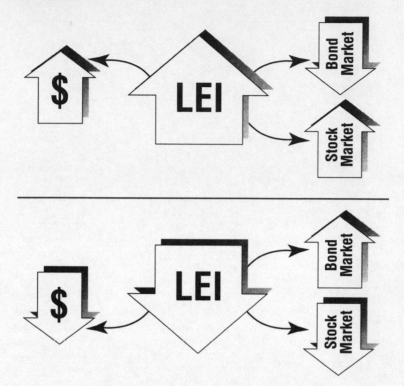

tor. For example, a higher than expected (more positive) reading triggers speculation that growth will be strong in coming months. The dollar moves higher on anticipated Federal Reserve tightening moves, whereas the bond market sells off. The reaction from stocks depends upon the current point in the economic cycle. As a general rule, early cycle signs of improvement in business activity are welcome by the equity markets which begin to factor in a more profitable economic environment. Late in the cycle, further strength is likely to be unwelcome, as fears mount about inflation and Federal Reserve restraint. ✿

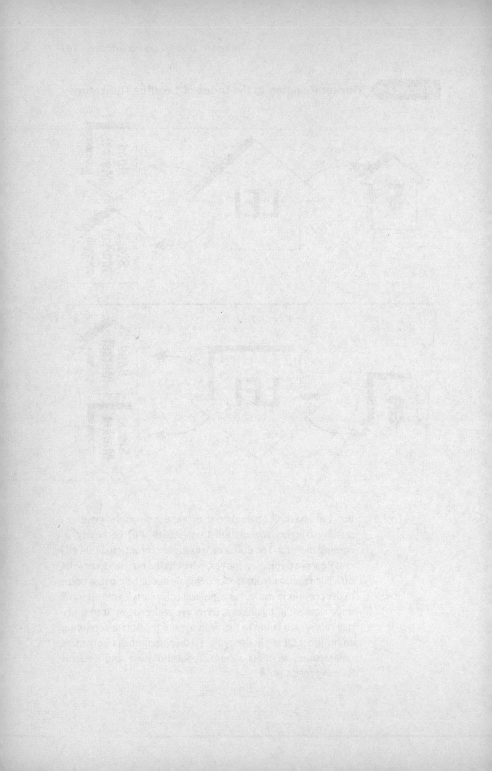

14

New Home Sales

The Heartbeat of America

Importance: ☆ ☆

Published by: **Bureau of the Census of the U.S. Department of Commerce**

Availability: **28th – 4th of the following month**

Frequency: **Monthly**

Volatility: **Moderate**

HOW THE MARKETS REACT:

Fixed-income:

NEW HOME SALES ⇑ ⇒ ⇓ BOND MARKET

NEW HOME SALES ⇓ ⇒ ⇑ BOND MARKET

Stock Market: NEW HOME SALES ⇒ NO REACTION

Dollar: NEW HOME SALES ⇒ NO REACTION

NOTEWORTHY CHARACTERISTICS:

✔ A leading indicator of economic activity — the first indicator to turn down when the economy goes into recession; the first to rise when it rebounds.

✔ Can be quite volatile, particularly during winter months.

HOME SALES ARE A LEADING INDICATOR
OF ECONOMIC ACTIVITY

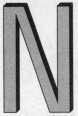 ew home sales are an important indicator of the degree of strength or weakness in the key housing sector of the economy. Housing is an extremely crucial segment of the economy because, historically, changes in consumer spending patterns have appeared first in autos and housing *(Fig. 14-1)*. Therefore, if the selling pace of new homes begins to slacken, then eventually housing starts begin to slow, and employment in the construction industry declines. Once the housing sector begins to slide, numerous related industries — like lumber and home furnishings — also begin to suffer. Thus, a drop-off in home sales can be a leading indicator of an impending recession. Similarly, when the economy begins to rebound, the housing and automobile sectors are usually the first to experience recovery.

DATA ARE PROVIDED FOR FOUR
GEOGRAPHIC AREAS

The Census Bureau provides monthly data on new home sales for the nation as a whole and for four geographical areas — the Northeast, the Midwest, the South, and the West. The data are collected from builders throughout the country and represent signed contracts — even though some contracts could fall through prior to closing.

THIS REPORT ALSO CONTAINS DATA ON HOUSE
PRICES AND UNSOLD HOMES

In addition to the data on home sales, there is information regarding the average and median sales prices, the number of houses for sale, and the supply of unsold homes (expressed as the number of months it would take at the current selling rate to eliminate all of the unsold homes). From this data, we acquire a reasonable sense of the state of the housing sector.

THESE DATA ARE VOLATILE

The problem with the home sales data is that they tend to be quite volatile. This obviously limits the data's usefulness. It

Figure 14-1 New Home Sales

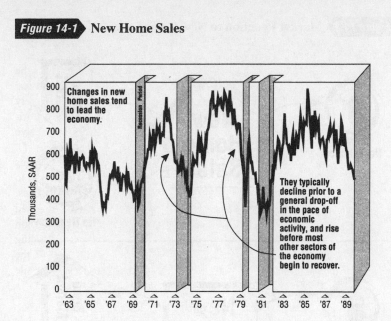

is usually best to look at a three-month moving average when trying to decipher changes in the growth-rate trend of this series. The data are usually published near month-end for the prior month.

IT IS HARD TO PREDICT HOME SALES, SO SURPRISES CAN OCCUR

Since they are so volatile, new home sales are difficult to predict. Volatility always adds the potential for surprise. When surprises occur, the home sales data may have a moderate impact on the fixed-income markets *(Fig. 14-2)*. However, traders and salespeople are aware of the volatility and tend to view these data cautiously.

A RISE IN SALES MAY PUSH THE BOND MARKET LOWER

Nevertheless, if home sales rise unexpectedly and market participants conclude that this is the beginning of a new trend, the participants react adversely and push interest rates higher. An unanticipated decline prompts the opposite response.

Figure 14-2 Market Reaction to New Home Sales

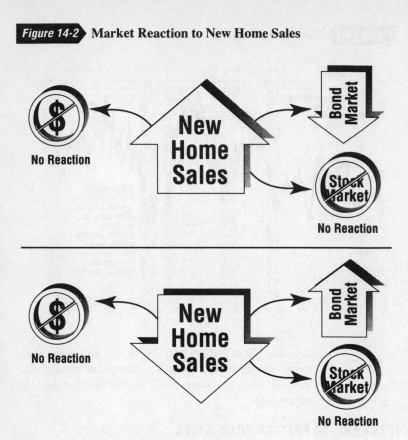

THE STOCK MARKET AND THE DOLLAR PROBABLY DO NOT REACT

The stock market and the foreign exchange markets do not appear to attach a great deal of importance to this report and, as a result, it is rare to decipher a reaction in either market. ✸

15

Construction Spending

20% of the Pie!

Importance:	☆ ☆
Published by:	**Bureau of the Census of the U.S. Department of Commerce**
Availability:	**1st business day of the month for two months prior**
Frequency:	**Monthly**
Volatility:	**High**

HOW THE MARKETS REACT:

Fixed-income:	**CONSTRUCTION SPENDING**	⇒ **NO REACTION**
Equity:	**CONSTRUCTION SPENDING**	⇒ **NO REACTION**
Dollar:	**CONSTRUCTION SPENDING**	⇒ **NO REACTION**

NOTEWORTHY CHARACTERISTICS:

✔ Represents about 20% of GNP.

✔ The revisions can sometimes be enormous!

CONSTRUCTION SPENDING PROVIDES INFORMATION ABOUT THREE SEPARATE GNP CATEGORIES

Construction spending measures the value of construction put in place during the course of that particular month. We are interested in it for two reasons. First, this report supplies us with information about three separate GNP categories that, combined, represent about 20% of GNP *(Fig. 15-1)*. For example, the nonresidential construction spending part of this report roughly approximates the nonresidential structures portion of the investment, or "I," component of GNP. Similarly, residential construction provides information about the residential component of investment. These two categories combined represent about 43% of "I" and about 8% of overall GNP. In addition, the public construction category tells us something regarding state and local government spending — another 11% of GNP — which, together with expenditures of the Federal government make up the "G" part of GNP. Thus, this report provides clues to the behavior of roughly 20% of GNP. That is quite sizeable!

Figure 15-1 **Construction Spending Versus GNP**

Construction Category	Percentage of GNP
1. Nonresidential Spending	3%
2. Residential Spending	5%
3. State and Local Government Spending	11%
	————
	19%

The construction spending report provides us with information concerning nearly 20% of GNP.

CHANGES IN THE CONSTRUCTION INDUSTRY
TEND TO LEAD THE ECONOMY

Second, economists frequently note that the automobile and construction industries are typically the first two sectors to go into recession when the bad times hit and are, pleasantly, the first two sectors to recover when conditions improve. Analysts faithfully track home and automobile sales for *hints* about when these changes are beginning to occur, and they revise their GNP forecasts accordingly. This report on construction spending provides an update on the state of the industry.

RESIDENTIAL, NONRESIDENTIAL AND
PUBLIC CONSTRUCTION ARE THE MOST
IMPORTANT CATEGORIES

Figure 15-2 summarizes the construction spending report for June 1990. It gives you an idea of the types of construction incorporated in this report. As the name suggests, the residential category includes single-family homes as well as apartment buildings. Nonresidential construction includes factories, offices, hotels and motels, churches, hospitals, and private schools. Public construction reflects expenditures on highways and streets, military reservations, water supply facilities, public school buildings, housing projects, and sewer systems.

CENSUS BUREAU TAPS A NUMBER OF
DIFFERENT SOURCES FOR THE DATA THEY NEED

The Census Bureau derives data on residential spending from its own surveys of housing starts and new home sales. Census looks to the F.W. Dodge Division of the McGraw Hill Information Systems Company to identify high-value nonresidential projects. The Bureau then selects a sample of these projects and requests monthly progress reports from the owners, builders, or architects responsible for these buildings. Similarly, the Census Bureau derives the public construction data from monthly progress reports from a sample of projects owned by state and local governments.

| Figure 15-2 | U.S. Construction Spending Levels, Current Dollars |

Value of New Construction Put in Place in the United States, Seasonally Adjusted Annual Rate

Source: U.S. Department of Commerce
Data in billions of current dollars

Release for: June 1990

The construction spending report has information separated into three major categories.

Type of Construction	June 1990	May 1990	April 1990	March 1990
Total New Construction	447.5	447.5	448.8	457.3
Private Construction	339.1	339.2	344.3	347.4
Residential Buildings	196.1	200.5	205.1	206.9
New Housing Units	132.1	136.0	140.5	145.3
One Unit Structures	111.3	115.3	120.1	125.3
Two or More Unit Structures	20.8	20.8	20.5	20.0
Nonresidential Buildings	107.1	103.1	104.0	104.9
Industrial	21.4	21.0	21.2	21.1
Office	26.9	24.4	25.3	25.9
Hotels and Motels	8.7	9.0	8.8	8.9
Other Commercial	30.4	30.2	30.5	31.3
Religious	3.0	2.9	2.7	2.7
Educational	3.6	3.5	3.7	3.4
Hospital and Institutional	8.8	8.0	7.7	7.3
Miscellaneous Buildings	4.3	4.1	4.2	4.2
Telephone and Telegraph	NA	9.6	9.4	9.4
All Other Private	3.3	3.1	3.1	3.4
Public Construction	108.4	108.5	104.5	109.9
Housing and Redevelopment	4.2	3.7	3.6	3.9
Industrial	1.6	1.1	1.5	1.8
Educational	19.7	20.0	18.4	19.4
Hospital	2.5	2.9	3.2	2.7
Other Public Buildings	17.5	16.8	16.5	16.2
Highways and Streets	29.7	30.7	29.8	32.4
Military Facilities	4.1	3.9	3.7	5.1
Conservation and Development	3.9	5.5	5.0.	5.0
Sewer Systems	10.5	10.3	10.7	10.5
Water Supply Facilities	5.2	4.7	4.2	4.4
Miscellaneous Public	9.4	8.8	7.9	8.5

THERE ARE TWO PROBLEMS WITH THE CONSTRUCTION SPENDING DATA

Unfortunately, there are two problems with this monthly report on construction spending. First, it is not very timely. It is released on the first business day of the month for two months prior. That makes it one of the *last* pieces of information we receive about the state of the economy for any given month. Since we have already seen 14 reports on various sectors of the economy, we basically know what has happened during that month. The incremental value of the 15th report is quite small. Second, the report tends to be quite volatile and revisions can be sizeable. With any of these volatile reports, economists are forced to work with year-over-year statistics, or three-month moving averages, in order to detect changes in trends. Thus, it takes three or four months before one can conclude that a trend rate of growth has been broken.

Figure 15-3 ▶ **Market Reaction to Construction Spending**

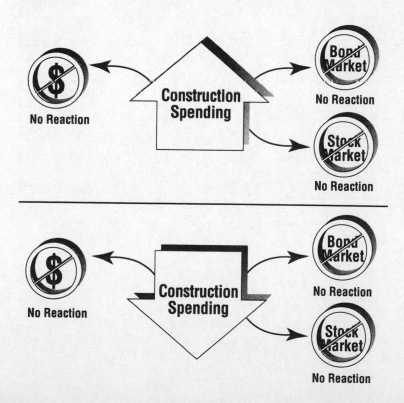

THE MARKETS IGNORE THIS REPORT

From a market point of view, this report is useless! The markets — all of them — essentially ignore it *(Fig. 15-3)*. This is probably because, as noted above, it is not very timely. Moreover, even when the data have been released, construction spending can be revised significantly a month later. You may legitimately ask why we bother to include this report in our review if the markets do not react to it. The answer is that the construction report helps the specialists achieve a better reading on GNP growth for the current quarter and, perhaps, for the quarter ahead. We noted earlier that the construction categories provide information on about 20% of GNP. That is too large a percentage to ignore, because *ultimately*, interest rate movements are going to be determined by what happens to GNP growth. ⬍

16

Factory Orders and Manufacturing Inventories

Durables Revisited

Importance:	☆
Published by:	Bureau of the Census of the U.S. Department of Commerce
Availability:	30th – 6th for two months prior
Frequency:	Monthly
Volatility:	Very High

HOW THE MARKETS REACT:

Fixed-income:	FACTORY ORDERS ⇑ ⇒ ⇓ BOND MARKET	
	FACTORY ORDERS ⇓ ⇒ ⇑ BOND MARKET	
Stock Market:	FACTORY ORDERS ⇒ NO REACTION	
Dollar:	FACTORY ORDERS ⇒ NO REACTION	

NOTEWORTHY CHARACTERISTICS:

✔ There is not much new information in this report.

THIS REPORT CONTAINS MORE DATA THAN THE PREVIOUSLY-RELEASED REPORT ON DURABLES

n many respects, this report is a rehash of the durable goods release that became available a week earlier. (The discussion of durables is contained in Chapter 11. We suggest that if you have not read that chapter yet, you do so now, as we only highlight the points made earlier.) However, the factory orders report merits review because it also contains data on orders and shipments of nondurable goods, manufacturing inventories, and the inventory/sales ratio. Furthermore, this report frequently contains significant revisions to the durable goods data. There have been instances when even the direction of change in orders has been revised from one week to the next — an initially reported increase of sizeable dimensions has turned into a decline, and vice versa.

The most important points made earlier are the following:

» Orders data are useful because they tell us something about the likely pace of production in the months ahead;
» They are extremely volatile and can fluctuate by three or four percentage points in any given month;
» They are subject to sizeable revisions; and
» They are very difficult to forecast.

IN ADDITION TO ORDERS FOR DURABLE GOODS, WE LEARN ABOUT ORDERS FOR NONDURABLES

This report on factory orders, shipments, and inventories becomes available about one week after the durable goods release. In addition to data on orders for durable goods — those products which have a useful life of more than three years, such as trains, planes, and automobiles, as well as refrigerators and stoves — this report tells us what happened to orders for nondurable goods. Many nondurables are essential commodities that we buy every month — food, clothing, and gasoline — and orders of such tend to be more stable. Thus, the fluctuation in this series on factory orders stems from its durable goods component.

WE ALSO RECEIVE DATA ON MANUFACTURING INVENTORIES

In addition to the revised data on orders and shipments of durables, and the inclusion of information on orders and shipments of nondurables, the most important new information is the data on manufacturing inventories. Inventories are important because they tell us something about what will happen to the economy in the months and quarters ahead.

Historically, the way the U.S. economy goes into recession is as follows:

» Sales begin to slump;
» Inventory levels start to climb; and
» Businesses sharply scale back production to trim unwanted inventories.

INVENTORIES ARE IMPORTANT BECAUSE A BUILDUP MAY CAUSE A RECESSION

The relationship between the change in business inventories and GNP growth is shown in *Figure 16-1*. The Commerce

Figure 16-1 ▶ **Change in Business Inventories**

In the past, an inventory buildup tended to be a precursor of recession.

This is less true today because of the computerization of inventories.

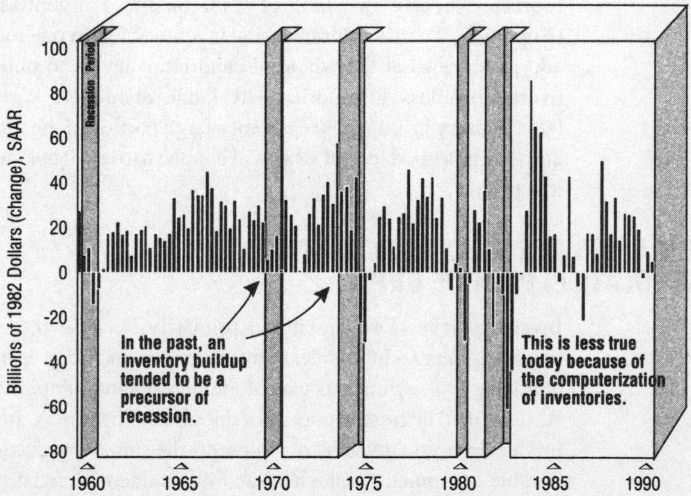

Department previously included the change in business inventories as one of the components of its leading indicators series. But when they revised this series in March 1989, Commerce dropped inventories and replaced it with other indicators. The reason was *not* that the inventories data are any less valuable as an indicator of future economic activity, but simply that they are not available in a timely enough manner to be incorporated in the initial release. When inventories were subsequently included one month later, the leading indicators series became subject to sizeable revisions. It is worth noting that we no longer see the same kinds of wild swings in business inventories that we saw in the 1950s, 1960s, and 1970s. Presumably this is happening because of the computerization of inventories. Many businesses are now able to determine instantly what their inventory levels are. As soon as a firm sees a slight rise, it quickly trims production to realign inventory levels with sales. Thus, in the years ahead, changes in business inventories may not be as reliable a guide to future GNP growth as they were previously because the swings will be less pronounced.

MANUFACTURING INVENTORIES REPRESENT NEARLY ONE-HALF OF THE TOTAL

This report tells us about manufacturing inventories which represent nearly one-half of total business inventories *(Fig. 16-2)*. To this manufacturing inventory figure one must add inventories at the wholesale and retail levels to obtain overall business inventories — available about two weeks later. Factory inventories represent a large portion of the total, and give us a good idea of what will happen to overall business inventories.

INVENTORIES ARE ALSO AN IMPORTANT (AND VOLATILE) PART OF GNP

Inventory levels are monitored primarily because the annualized *change* in business inventories is included in the quarterly GNP estimate as part of the investment component. As described in the GNP portion of this book (Chapter 2), gross private domestic investment represents the sum of producers' durable equipment, residential and nonresidential construc-

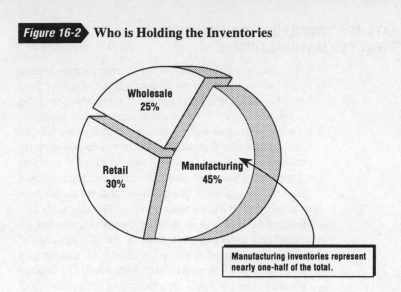

Figure 16-2 Who is Holding the Inventories

Wholesale
25%

Retail
30%

Manufacturing
45%

Manufacturing inventories represent
nearly one-half of the total.

tion, and the change in business inventories. Therefore, knowledge of manufacturing inventories can give us a clue concerning the overall change in business inventories, which is an integral part of the investment component of GNP.

THE INVENTORY TO SALES RATIO IS A LAGGING INDICATOR

Given the data on both manufacturing inventories and sales, we can calculate the inventory/sales ratio. This ratio is a lagging indicator of the economy because, historically, inventory levels continue to rise long after sales growth comes to a halt. However, most economists use this ratio to anticipate changes in the rate of inventory accumulation. For example, at some point after the trough of a recession, this ratio reaches an extremely low level. At this juncture one can expect manufacturers to accelerate their rate of inventory accumulation simply to keep pace with a growing volume of sales. Similarly, when the economy begins to contract, the inventory/sales ratio rises for several more months. But at some point companies become uncomfortable with the relationship between inventories and sales. As they cut back production, inventory levels are reduced and the ratio begins to fall.

DATA ARE COMPILED FROM AN EXTENSIVE SURVEY OF MANUFACTURERS

These data on orders, shipments and inventories are compiled by the Census Bureau of the Department of Commerce from a monthly survey of approximately 5,000 manufacturers from a universe of some 70,000 establishments. Most manufacturers with 1,000 or more employees are included, plus a selected sample of smaller companies. The survey respondents are categorized by industry; totals are then expanded to represent the universe of manufacturers. The orders data represent firm orders for immediate or future delivery that are documented by a signed contract or a letter of intent. The shipments data represent the sum total of sales for that month, whether for domestic use or for export. Inventories reflect book values of merchandise on hand at the end of the month, according to the valuation method used by each respondent. The data are released by the Census Bureau either just before the end of the month for the month prior, or just after the start of the following month.

THE MARKETS GENERALLY DO NOT REACT TO THIS REPORT — THE MYSTERY WAS REMOVED ONE WEEK EARLIER

For the most part, the fixed-income markets do not respond to this particular report *(Fig. 16-3)*. The reason is simple — the mystery surrounding the data is largely removed by the release of the durable goods report the previous week. Nondurable goods orders and shipments are quite steady and easy to predict. Thus, the only time that the markets react is on those occasions when the data on durable goods orders revises significantly, *or* when there is a surprising change in inventories. In that event, stronger-than-expected GNP growth causes interest rates to rise as market participants worry about higher inflation and/or a Federal Reserve tightening move.

Because the changes in this report are generally well-anticipated, the stock market and the dollar are rarely affected in any significant way. ✦

Figure 16-3 Market Reaction to Factory Orders

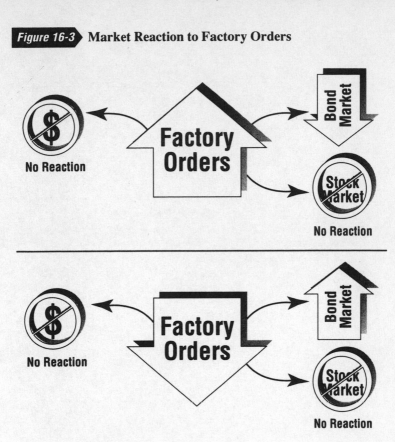

17

Business Inventories and Sales

You Have Heard It All Before!

Importance: ☆

Published by: **Bureau of the Census of the U.S. Department of Commerce**

Availability: **13th – 17th for two months prior**

Frequency: **Monthly**

Volatility: **Moderate**

HOW THE MARKETS REACT:

Fixed-income:
BUSINESS INVENTORIES ⇑ ⇒ UNCERTAIN
BUSINESS INVENTORIES ⇓ ⇒ UNCERTAIN

Stock Market:
BUSINESS INVENTORIES ⇒ NO REACTION

Dollar:
BUSINESS INVENTORIES ⇒ NO REACTION

NOTEWORTHY CHARACTERISTICS:

✔ None.

MOST OF THE DATA IN THIS REPORT HAVE ALREADY BEEN RELEASED

This report on business inventories and sales is a logical extension of several previously released reports — the durable goods data (which contains information on the sales of durable goods by manufacturers), the report on factory orders, shipments, and inventories, the retail sales report, and the wholesale inventories and sales data. (Durables, factory orders, and retail sales are detailed in Chapters 11, 16, and 7. We suggest that if you have not done so already, read those sections now, because our comments in this chapter are relatively brief.) The data on wholesale inventories and sales are not discussed in this book because they are never picked up by the press and, therefore, generate no market response. However, they are available about one week prior to the publication date of the business inventories report. From these earlier releases, we know what happened to inventories and sales at both the factory and wholesale stages of production. We also know what happened to retail sales. The only new item in this report is retail inventories.

BUSINESS INVENTORIES ARE AN IMPORTANT PART OF THE "I" COMPONENT OF GNP

We are interested in business inventories for two reasons. First, they are an important part of the investment component of GNP and, second, they provide further clues regarding the likely direction of the economy in the months ahead.

Gross private domestic investment, the "I" component in GNP, includes both residential and nonresidential construction spending, expenditures on producers' durable equipment, and the change in business inventories. Recall that GNP is a measure of *production*. Since we calculate GNP by adding up various types of sales data, it is necessary to add the change in business inventories to determine the actual level of production. For example, if a firm produces 100 toasters but sells only 90, the remaining 10 show up as an increase in inventories *(Fig. 17-1)*. If we attempt to measure GNP by adding up the *sales* data, we will calculate GNP as 90 *unless* we make some allowance for the increase in inventories. Similarly, if

| Figure 17-1 | The Change in Business Inventories and the GNP Calculation |

To estimate GNP from sales data, we must add the change in inventories.

1. All goods that are produced must either be sold or added to inventories.

2. GNP measures the dollar amount of goods produced.

Sales	+	Change in Inventories	=	GNP
90		+10	=	100
90		−10	=	80

3. But if we simply add up several types of spending (or sales) data, we will not estimate GNP correctly.

4. To get the correct answer for GNP, we must add the change in business inventories to the sales data.

a company continues to sell 90 toasters the following year, but only produces 80 in an effort to bring inventory levels into closer alignment with sales, we will not arrive at the correct figure for GNP and production (80) unless we adjust the sales data (90) for the change in toaster inventories (−10).

BUSINESS INVENTORIES ARE ALSO AN IMPORTANT BAROMETER OF FUTURE ECONOMIC ACTIVITY

We noted, in the chapter on factory orders, shipments, and inventories, that one reason the U.S. economy slides into recession is because business inventories rise in response to slumping sales — eventually forcing businesses to cut production to trim unwanted stocks. Aside from the GNP accounting aspect, businesses seem slow to recognize that inventories are reaching dangerous levels until well after the fact. Thus, inventory *levels* tend to be a *lagging* indicator of economic activity. They do not begin to decline (or rise) until well after the peak (or trough) of the business cycle has been attained. The *change* in business inventories, however, begins to slow as the economy approaches a peak, and starts to climb as the economy nears the trough of a recession. For this reason, the *change* in business inventories is a *leading* indicator of GNP growth. In fact, until March 1989, the Commerce Department incorporated the change in their index of leading indicators. But because it was never available in a timely manner, and gave rise to substantial revisions when it was included a month later, Commerce decided to drop the change in business inventories in favor of other series. Nevertheless, it continues to be a reasonably good leading indicator. *Figure 17-2* shows how the change in business inventories has foreshadowed GNP growth over the course of the past 30 years. It should be noted that the widespread implementation of inventory control procedures (e.g., "just-in-time" inventories) during the 1980s significantly reduced the volume of inventories that firms were required to hold for any given amount of sales. Furthermore, it dampened considerably the volatility of inventories. Throughout that period, we did not see the dramatic swings in inventories that we had become accustomed to seeing in other decades. Thus, it is likely that, in the years ahead, inventory changes will not be as important a harbinger of business cycle changes.

Figure 17-2 **Change in Business Inventories**

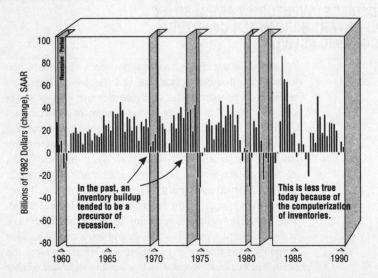

BUSINESS SALES ARE MORE OR LESS A CONTEMPORANEOUS INDICATOR OF THE ECONOMY

The Commerce Department includes this series in its monthly index of coincident indicators — it begins to turn up and decline roughly in sync with business cycle troughs and peaks. If we begin to suspect that the economy is about to enter a recession, for example, we can use business sales to confirm or refute that notion.

FROM THIS REPORT WE CAN CALCULATE THE RATIO OF INVENTORIES TO SALES

In our earlier discussion, we noted that companies adjust inventory levels to keep them in close alignment with sales. The way that economists determine whether inventories are consistent with sales is by calculating the Inventory/Sales ratio. *Figure 17-3* gives you some idea of how this ratio fluctuates throughout the course of the business cycle. You

Figure 17-3 **Ratio of Business Inventories to Business Final Sales (Quarterly)**

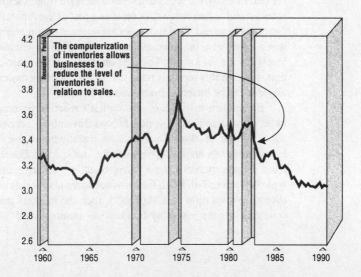

The computerization of inventories allows businesses to reduce the level of inventories in relation to sales.

can see quite clearly that the computerization of inventories during the 1980s allowed firms to reduce inventory levels in relationship to sales and we expect this process to continue.

THE DATA ARE COMPILED FROM A MONTHLY SURVEY

The data on business inventories and sales are published by the Census Bureau of the Department of Commerce from a monthly survey of manufacturers' shipments, inventories, and orders, and from the merchant wholesalers and retail trade surveys. They are published around the middle of the month for two months earlier. Thus, these data only become available after a considerable lag.

THIS IS ANOTHER REPORT THAT DOES NOT GENERATE ANY SIGNIFICANT MARKET REACTION

The markets do not pay much attention to this report because so much of the underlying data is already available and, as a result, surprises are rare *(Fig. 17-4)*. For example, *all* of the sales data have been published previously. Retail sales data for that month were released almost a month earlier; factory sales are published two weeks prior as a part of the report on factory orders; and wholesale sales are released the preceding week. Similarly, manufacturing and wholesale inventories levels are already known. Thus, the only piece of information that is new in this report is retail inventories — but occasionally this can be different from what we expect.

Even when that occurs, the market's reaction is sometimes difficult to gauge. As noted above, inventories account for a portion of GNP. Therefore, an unanticipated rise in inventory levels boosts GNP growth for that quarter. For the fixed income markets, faster GNP growth is a negative and, typically, prices fall. But if that inventory gain also boosts the inventory/sales ratio to a high level, then the markets may conclude that the inventory buildup was *unintentional* — in

Figure 17-4 ▸ **Market Reaction to Business Inventories**

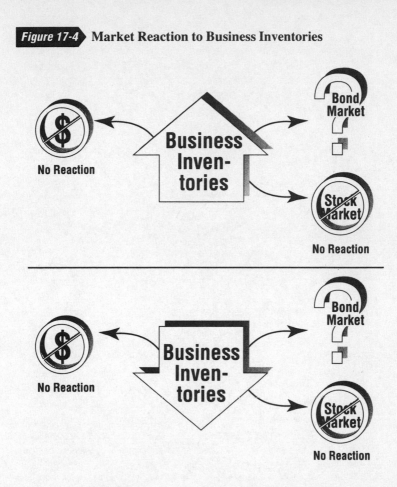

which case businesses have to scale back production in the months ahead, thereby producing slower GNP growth. Viewed in this manner, a rise in inventory levels can be construed as a positive event for the fixed income markets. For the stock market and the foreign exchange markets, this report is usually a nonevent. ⬇

18
Merchandise Trade Balance
Wheat for Caviar

Importance: ☆☆

Published by: **Bureau of the Census of the the U.S. Department of Commerce**

Availability: **15th – 17th for two months prior**

Frequency: **Monthly**

Volatility: **Moderate**

HOW THE MARKETS REACT:

TRADE BALANCE ⇑ ⇒ UNCERTAIN
(i.e., deficit becomes less negative)

Fixed-income:

EXPORTS ⇑ ⇒ ⇓ BOND MARKET
IMPORTS ⇑ ⇒ ⇓ BOND MARKET
EXPORTS ⇓ ⇒ ⇑ BOND MARKET
IMPORTS ⇓ ⇒ ⇑ BOND MARKET

Equity:

TRADE BALANCE ⇑ ⇒ ⇑ STOCK MARKET
TRADE BALANCE ⇓ ⇒ ⇓ STOCK MARKET

Dollar:

TRADE BALANCE ⇑ ⇒ ⇑ DOLLAR
TRADE BALANCE ⇓ ⇒ ⇓ DOLLAR

NOTEWORTHY CHARACTERISTICS:

✔ The trade data are of increasing importance.
✔ The market's reaction to the data is very difficult to determine.

THE IMPORTANCE OF THE TRADE SECTOR HAS GROWN

Prior to 1980s, the U.S. economy tended to be viewed as "closed" since the trade sector accounted for a rather small portion of overall production and demand — around 7% of GNP in 1970. But, large swings in exchange rates — following the breakup of Bretton Woods in the early 1970s — and steady growth in world trade have forced the United States to deal with a sector largely ignored. Moreover, heightened competition for global markets, symbolized by Japan's race for market share, has generated a new awareness of trade-related issues. As shown in *Figure 18-1*, the trade sector currently accounts for approximately 13% of GNP — and this percentage will move higher in the 1990s as trade with eastern Europe expands.

Figure 18-1 ▶ **The Importance of the Trade Sector Has Grown**

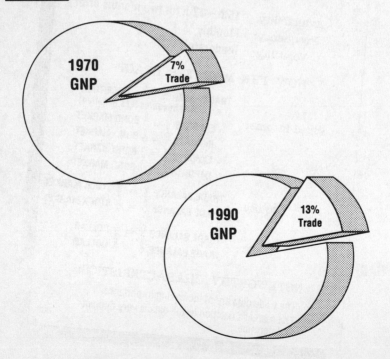

CHANGES IN THE VALUE OF THE DOLLAR HAVE AN IMPORTANT IMPACT ON THE TRADE DEFICIT

Cause and effect regarding exchange rates and trade flows are sometimes difficult to decipher. However, the surging dollar from 1980 to 1985 had a pronounced negative impact upon the U.S. trade balance, as *Figure 18-2* clearly demonstrates. As the deficits widened to alarming proportions, actions taken by U.S. policymakers — along with economic fundamentals — served to effectively devalue the dollar. Since 1986, the dollar's retreat has helped redress some of these imbalances, although structural problems remain.

Figure 18-2 The U.S. Merchandise Trade Deficit Versus the Trade-weighted Value of the Dollar

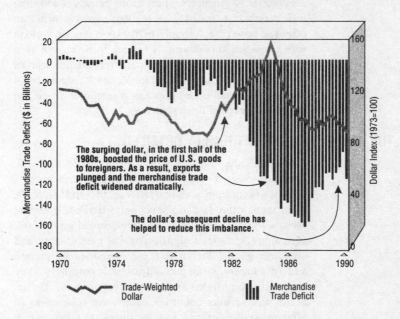

The surging dollar, in the first half of the 1980s, boosted the price of U.S. goods to foreigners. As a result, exports plunged and the merchandise trade deficit widened dramatically.

The dollar's subsequent decline has helped to reduce this imbalance.

Trade-Weighted Dollar   Merchandise Trade Deficit

TRADE BALANCE = EXPORTS – IMPORTS

Reduced to its essentials, the monthly trade balance is rather straightforward: it represents the dollar value difference between U.S. exports and imports on a seasonally adjusted basis. Recently, the deficit has been running about $8 billion per month — and at one point was averaging almost twice that amount. Even though America is in the midst of an export boom, imports continue to rise as well. Assuming *very* optimistic growth rates of 10% for exports and only 5% for imports, it would take almost five years for the United States to register a trade surplus. The reason for this is that the *absolute* amount of exports, currently about $33 billion each month, is swamped by imports of approximately $41 billion.

WHAT IS IMPORTANT IS WHETHER THE DEFICIT IS EXPANDING OR SHRINKING

From a GNP accounting standpoint, exports add to GNP while imports must be subtracted from GNP, since a portion of U.S. consumption and investment demand is satisfied by foreign — not domestic — producers. Thus, during periods of widening trade deficits, the United States registers slower growth than otherwise is the case. Recently, hefty export demand — along with an import slowdown — is serving to boost GNP even though the United States still runs an overall deficit with its trading partners. What is critical from a GNP standpoint is not whether the overall trade balance is in surplus or deficit, but whether it is expanding or shrinking.

THE TRADE DATA ARE EXTREMELY DETAILED

Each month, the Census Bureau gathers data on total U.S. exports (wheat, computers, and tractors) and imports (Toyotas, fax machines, and caviar) *(Fig. 18-3* and *Fig. 18-4)*. Even though the data are amazingly detailed, investors are advised to focus on the following broad groups: oil, agriculture, industrial supplies, capital goods, autos, and consumer goods. Trends in these categories are plotted and investment strategies adjusted accordingly. The report also highlights trade flows between the United States and various countries, which are referred to as bilateral trade deficits and surpluses. For the record, America's largest trading partner is not Japan, Germany, or Britain; it is Canada. As indicated on *Figure 18-5*, our northern neighbor accounts for almost 20% of total U.S. trade, followed closely by Japan. Mexico, Germany, and the United Kingdom each represent about 5% of the total.

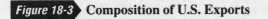 **Composition of U.S. Exports**

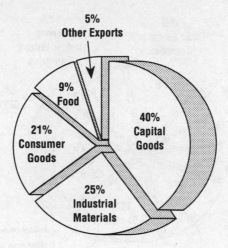

**5%
Other Exports**

**9%
Food**

**21%
Consumer
Goods**

**40%
Capital
Goods**

**25%
Industrial
Materials**

Figure 18-4 **Composition of U.S. Imports**

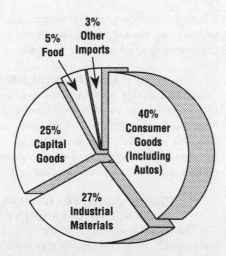

**3%
Other
Imports**

**5%
Food**

**25%
Capital
Goods**

**40%
Consumer
Goods
(Including
Autos)**

**27%
Industrial
Materials**

Figure 18-5 U.S. Trading Partners: Exports Plus Imports

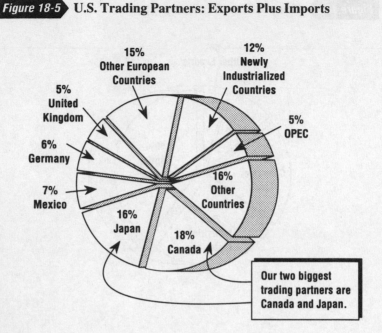

15% Other European Countries

12% Newly Industrialized Countries

5% United Kingdom

5% OPEC

6% Germany

7% Mexico

16% Other Countries

16% Japan

18% Canada

Our two biggest trading partners are Canada and Japan.

THERE ARE FOUR SEPARATE REPORTS ON TRADE

It is important to recognize that there are four separate reports on trade, and market participants need to know which are important and which are not *(Fig. 18-6).*

MERCHANDISE TRADE DEFICIT

From a market viewpoint, the most valuable of these trade reports is the monthly merchandise trade balance because it is the most timely — all the others are released quarterly. It is important to note that the monthly trade figures are for *merchandise* only. Services, investment income, and military aid are not taken into account in these figures.

MERCHANDISE TRADE DEFICIT — BALANCE OF PAYMENTS BASIS

The second trade report to appear is the merchandise trade deficit on a "balance of payments" basis. Market

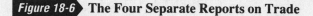

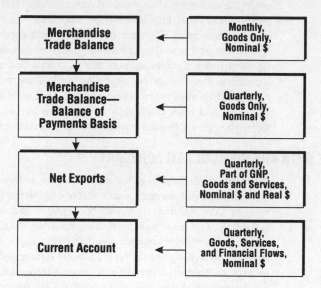

Figure 18-6 The Four Separate Reports on Trade

| Merchandise Trade Balance | ← | Monthly, Goods Only, Nominal $ |

| Merchandise Trade Balance— Balance of Payments Basis | ← | Quarterly, Goods Only, Nominal $ |

| Net Exports | ← | Quarterly, Part of GNP, Goods and Services, Nominal $ and Real $ |

| Current Account | ← | Quarterly, Goods, Services, and Financial Flows, Nominal $ |

participants can disregard this report. It essentially re-hashes the monthly data (excluding military trade along with a few other technical adjustments) and never generates any market response.

NET EXPORTS

The third trade-related report, however, is important. Data from this report is contained in the GNP figure and is known as "net exports." Until this release, all our trade information has been with respect to goods; now we have our first look at exports and imports of services. It is at this point that analysts examine the entire trade sector, represented by $(X - M)$ in the GNP equation. These data are presented in both nominal and real (inflation-adjusted) terms. What we find is that services exports considerably exceed services imports — thus, there is a sizable surplus in the services account which offsets a significant portion of the deficit in merchandise trade.

CURRENT ACCOUNT

The final report is known as the "current account." Curiously, the markets tend to ignore this report. But, in fact, it is probably the most important of all trade data — it is the broadest measure of U.S. trade and includes both goods and services, as well as unilateral transfers (i.e., foreign aid) and financial flows. Current account data is crucial because it represents the amount of trade that must somehow be financed. However, when foreigners find U.S. investment attractive, and more funds flow in than flow abroad, this foreign investment finances a portion of our net export deficit.

TRADE DATA ARE DIFFICULT TO FORECAST

Trade data are difficult to gather and to forecast, and we have learned to live with the many data collection problems. However, the Census Bureau figures are becoming more accurate and timely. Likewise, economists are improving their forecasts of imports by examining customs duties data — taxes collected on arriving goods. Yet the process is more difficult for exports. Analysts often take a "bottom up" approach, e.g., did Boeing actually deliver its jets within a certain month? Despite the uncertainties, a broad consensus is formed, against which the market judges a particular trade report.

A DECLINE IN THE TRADE DEFICIT WILL BOOST THE DOLLAR

How are the major markets affected? *(Fig. 18-7)* Let us begin with the dollar since its response is usually the most direct. A decline in the deficit is always welcome news for holders of the greenback — one must *buy* dollars to purchase U.S. exports and *sell* dollars to buy imports. In this case, expectations play a major role. Suppose the "Street" consensus places the June trade deficit at $8 billion. A $5 billion shortfall is viewed, perhaps even seized upon, as an opportunity to buy the dollar, short the yen, or sell sterling. We concede, however, that the foreign exchange market has become less impressed with trade reports than they used to be. Generally speaking, if the dollar has been trading within a well-defined range, the monthly trade figures tend to be ignored beyond a few hours. Conversely, if the dollar has just broken out of its recent boundaries, data on trade flows have a greater impact.

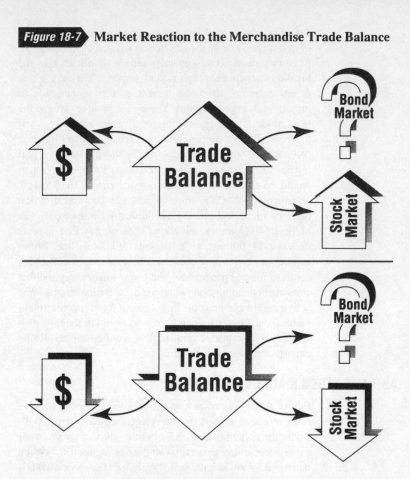

Figure 18-7 Market Reaction to the Merchandise Trade Balance

BONDS CAN GO EITHER WAY — DEPENDING UPON THEIR MOOD AT THE MOMENT

The case for bond investors is a little more subtle. Suppose the trade deficit comes in less than expected. Bond investors are torn between two factors. First, a smaller deficit triggers a dollar rally — good news for bond market participants. But, if the trade deficit is shrinking, it simultaneously adds to GNP growth. A faster pace of economic activity is negative for bonds. What should an investor do? It is not always clear — the market reaction seems to be determined by the mood of the moment. In all candor, there are times when economists would have had a hard time anticipating the market's response even if we had known the numbers in advance! Caveats aside, fixed-income analysts generally attach significance to the breakdown between exports and imports. Given a lower deficit scenario, the bond market prefers a reduction in imports to a surge in exports. The reason revolves around the bond holder's ever-present fear of a strong economy — and the possibility of higher inflation. Recall, exports increase GNP whereas imports reduce GNP. In short, a dream report (again, taking into account expectations) for bond investors would be the following: (1) Prior to release, the "Street" assumes an $8 billion trade deficit. (2) The actual deficit narrows to $5 billion. (3) The dollar is immediately bid higher. (4) Upon examination, it turns out that exports *declined* $1 billion, while imports fell $4 billion. Softer exports imply less pressure on manufacturers' demand for credit to finance production, and lower imports suggest that consumer spending is slowing — a deceleration in economic activity is always welcome by holders of fixed-income instruments. A nightmare for bond investors would be the reverse — a higher than expected trade deficit, a dollar sell-off, strong exports and even stronger imports.

AND THE STOCK MARKET WILL RALLY

Equity players are often torn between following the bond or foreign exchange markets. Many times a trade report is bullish for the dollar but bearish for bonds — or vice versa. In our experience, stocks generally end the day higher if the deficit narrowed, or lower if the deficit widened. The stock market's response is also a function of whether the "trade problem" is a major issue at the time. If not, the best strategy for long-term investors is to follow *industry trends*, both on the export and import side. This requires some study and cannot be acted upon in a half hour. But patience is sometimes rewarded. Those who caught the turning point in 1988 happily noted rising share prices of firms with export exposure. Many of the companies that had been pronounced "DOA" were busy recapturing overseas markets — and returning to profitability. ‡

Part III
Federal Reserve
Operations

19

Overview of Federal Reserve Policy

Its Determination and Implementation

n this book's introduction we pointed out that the Federal Reserve (the "Fed") has an enormous impact on the economy through its control of key interest rates. Combined with its power to create money, the Fed's policies greatly influence commodity prices, the value of the U.S. dollar in foreign exchange markets, government and corporate bond yields, mortgage rates, real estate prices, and stock market valuations. With the demise of coherent fiscal policy, the Federal Reserve has effectively taken over management of the business cycle. Unless you have some feel for monetary policy and a fundamental macroeconomic outlook, you will be forever "surprised" by events. Moreover, investing in the 1990s will require a global view. As the markets become increasingly interconnected, a better grasp of monetary policies overseas will be needed, especially if an investor wishes to diversify outside the home market. Understanding the Federal Reserve will help you comprehend the workings of other central banks, such as the Bundesbank and the Bank of Japan.

The following two chapters focus on practical aspects of "Fed-watching" that can be utilized by those involved in the financial markets. Investors, traders, and speculators must understand exactly what the Federal Reserve does and does not control, what the federal funds rate means and its relation to other interest rates, how policies are implemented, what economic data the Fed monitors, and so forth.

MARKET PARTICIPANTS MUST UNDERSTAND HOW THE FEDERAL RESERVE DETERMINES MONETARY POLICY

Chapter 20 arms the reader with a working knowledge of the central bank and how it operates in the marketplace — its stated goals and real-world agenda, the relationship between the Fed and other branches of government, and how policy shifts affect the fixed-income market. We analyze the various

monetary aggregates and the impact they have on GNP growth
and on inflation. We also discuss the tools that the Fed has at
its disposal and how they actually bring about changes in the
economy. A great deal of emphasis is placed on the macroeconomic environment. Now that you are armed with detailed
knowledge of the economic indicators, from housing starts to
the PPI, the next chapter serves to reinforce these concepts
*because the Federal Reserve follows these very same data! If
you want to know what the Fed is up to, simply watch what
they watch.*

KNOWLEDGE OF HOW THE FEDERAL RESERVE IMPLEMENTS POLICY IS EQUALLY IMPORTANT

In addition to monitoring factors which help *determine*
Federal Reserve policy — overall economic activity, employment growth, the inflation rate, etc. — traders and investors
need to know how the Fed *implements* monetary policy. In
Chapter 21, we take a more detailed look at the "plumbing" —
how the Fed attempts to hit its funds rate target, the nuts and
bolts of the reserves market, why the central bank may choose
customer repos rather than system repos, and (perhaps most
importantly) how you can tell when the Fed is in the process
of changing policy. The Fed is constantly sending signals to
the markets about the desired level of short-term rates. If we
appreciate how they carry out their operations, we can quickly
focus on those occasions when the central bank is about to
change course. This is especially useful for those of you who
make a living trading and managing money, and for investors
who want to know how and why Fed policies are actually
carried out. ✦

20

Determining Monetary Policy

The Basics

ALL POLICY-MAKERS SEEK RAPID GNP GROWTH, FULL EMPLOYMENT, AND STABLE PRICES

To refresh your memory, here is the classroom version of governmental policy-making. Note that there is nothing wrong here, it is just incomplete. The ultimate objective of both fiscal and monetary policy is to achieve an economy characterized by GNP growth, relatively full employment and stable prices.

By altering government spending and taxation, thereby influencing aggregate demand, *fiscal* policy has a significant impact on economic activity, employment, and the rate of inflation. The responsibility for implementing fiscal policy is shared between the White House and Congress.

In 1913, Congress created the Federal Reserve system for the purpose of carrying out *monetary* policy. By regulating the volume of bank reserves through its open market operations, the Federal Reserve influences interest rates — the level of which causes changes in the behavior of businesses and consumers *(Fig. 20-1)*. Policy changes also affect the pace of

Figure 20-1 How Federal Reserve Monetary Policy Affects the Economy and Inflation

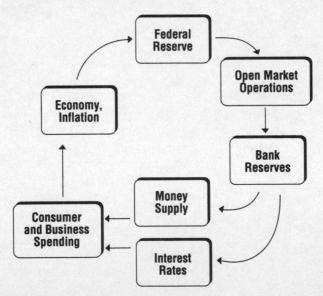

money creation, ultimately affecting economic activity and prices. In a recession, defined as at least two consecutive quarters of negative GNP growth, the Federal Reserve acts to stimulate credit expansion by increasing bank reserves, prompting interest rates to fall *(Fig. 20-2)*. An increased amount of loanable funds thus becomes available for business and consumer borrowing. As business activity picks up, firms increase hiring, and the unemployment rate falls. In an inflationary period when the CPI is running at a 5% rate or higher and the economy is booming, the Federal Reserve acts to cool the economy by decreasing bank reserves. With fewer funds available, interest rates tend to rise. These higher rates discourage borrowers — both corporate and consumer — and retard economic activity. At some point, slower growth results in moderating price pressures.

Figure 20-2 **The Federal Reserve and the Economy**

When the Federal Reserve wants to Stimulate the Economy

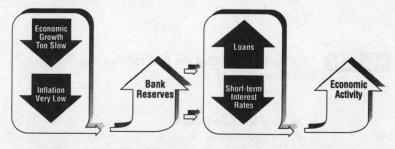

When the Federal Reserve wants to Constrain the Economy

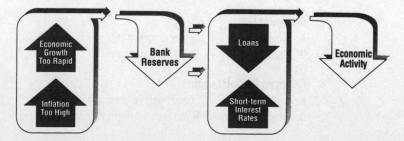

THE FEDERAL RESERVE CAN IMPLEMENT POLICY IN THREE WAYS

There are three ways the Federal Reserve can implement monetary policy and influence the level of interest rates.

OPEN MARKET OPERATIONS

Through its Federal Open Market Committee (FOMC), the Federal Reserve controls a portfolio of government securities, mainly U.S. Treasury bills, notes, and bonds *(Fig. 20-3)*. If the Fed buys securities, it pays for them with funds that are deposited in commercial banks' accounts at the Federal Reserve. This action is expansionary since it increases bank reserves and adds to the availability of loanable funds, which cause interest rates to decline. Conversely, if the Fed sells securities, the funds to pay for them come from those same commercial bank accounts. This action is contractionary, as it reduces the reserves that banks have available for loans, and interest rates rise. About 80% of the time, the Federal Reserve executes a change in monetary policy by altering its open market operations.

Figure 20-3 The Three Tools that the Federal Reserve Uses to Implement Policy

1. **Open Market Operations**
   A. Expansionary — Buy U.S. Treasury securities and increase reserves
   B. Contractionary — Sell U.S. Treasury securities and decrease reserves

2. **Discount Rate**
   A. Expansionary — Lower discount rate
   B. Contractionary — Raise discount rate

3. **Reserve Requirements**
   A. Expansionary — Lower reserve requirements
   B. Contractionary — Raise reserve requirements

DISCOUNT RATE

Adjusting the discount rate is another tool available to the Federal Reserve. The discount rate is the interest rate charged to member banks when they borrow directly from the Federal Reserve. When the discount rate is raised (or lowered), almost all other short-term interest rates rise (or fall). This occurs because a change in the discount rate is by far the most visible of all the Federal Reserve's monetary policy tools; it makes front-page headlines on every newspaper in the country. When the central bank alters the discount rate, the markets correctly interpret that action as a major policy statement.

RESERVE REQUIREMENTS

Raising or lowering the reserve requirement — the percentage of deposits that banks are required to hold as non-interest-bearing assets — is another way the Federal Reserve can influence the level of interest rates. If banks are forced to maintain a larger portion of their assets as reserves, they have less money to make mortgages or other loans. This tool of monetary policy is talked about a lot in theory, but is rarely used. Most recently, the Federal Reserve decided to drop the reserve requirement on bank CDs and Eurocurrency deposits in order to bolster bank profitability. This change, however, was the first in seven years.

THE FUNDS RATE IS THE BEST GAUGE OF FEDERAL RESERVE POLICY

Since bank reserves earn no interest, banks generally like to keep no more than the required minimum on deposit at their local Federal Reserve bank or in their vaults. However, because deposit flows are constantly shifting, reserves shortages and surpluses are routinely encountered. Banks with excess reserves lend them to banks with reserve deficits *(Fig. 20-4)*. There is an active market for these loanable funds, and the "price" paid for their use — the interest rate charged — is known as the *federal funds rate*. Market participants use this (primarily overnight) rate as a barometer not only of existing conditions within the banking industry, but of the Federal Reserve's position on credit and money growth. A rising funds rate is usually indicative of a contractionary monetary policy designed to decrease the availability of credit. A decline in this key rate suggests an expansionary policy.

Figure 20-4 How the Federal Funds Market Works

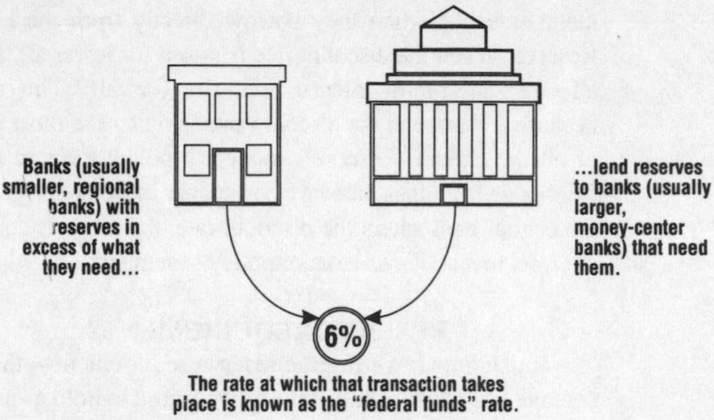

Banks (usually smaller, regional banks) with reserves in excess of what they need...

...lend reserves to banks (usually larger, money-center banks) that need them.

6%

The rate at which that transaction takes place is known as the "federal funds" rate.

THE FEDERAL RESERVE SEEKS A STRONG ECONOMY, MINIMAL INFLATION, AND FULL EMPLOYMENT

The Federal Reserve's general goals and basic policy tools are a good starting point, but they do not tell us much. All branches of government wish (presumably) for a strong economy, minimal inflation and low unemployment. But equally important, at least for Congress and Administration officials, are the prospects of being re-elected.

THE RELATIVE IMPORTANCE OF THESE GOALS CAN CHANGE OVER TIME

Depending on the economic environment, certain goals take precedence over others. For example, in the 1970s, the chief political worry was inflation. Even though unemployment trended higher for most of the decade, the public wanted "something done" about rising prices. This brought forth a host of quick fixes, such as Nixon's wage and price "freeze" and Carter's oil price "guidelines." Naturally, the government never considered reducing its own spending since constituents continued to demand entitlements, nuclear weapons, and water projects. Not surprisingly, voters refrained from mounting a vigorous lobbying campaign to raise taxes. As the crisis came to a head in the summer of 1979, President Carter was more or less forced into appointing an inflation "hawk" to head the central bank. His name, of course, was Paul Volcker. Acting swiftly, the new Federal Reserve chairman instituted what amounted to a frontal assault on spiraling prices. With inflation rates once again headed toward double-digits, Volcker signaled a dramatic change in policy on October 6, 1979.

First, the Federal Reserve hiked the discount rate by a full percentage point, from 11% to 12%. Second, the chairman established an 8% marginal reserve requirement on "managed liabilities," effectively halting a method by which banks had brought about rapid credit expansion. Finally (and perhaps most importantly), the Federal Reserve Board placed "...greater emphasis, in day-to-day operations, on the supply of bank reserves, and less emphasis on confining short-term fluctuations in the federal funds rate." In other words, the Federal Reserve began targeting (and squeezing) bank reserves and money growth directly — even if that meant substantially higher interest rates.

FEDERAL RESERVE POLICY IS INDEPENDENT OF BOTH CONGRESS AND THE ADMINISTRATION — BUT IT IS SENSITIVE TO THE WISHES OF BOTH

This experience in the late 1970s and early 1980s is a good example of the practical distinction between monetary and fiscal policy. Given the reality of politics, there is little chance that either Congress or the Administration — even if they have the power to do so — can take such unpopular steps. This is not to say that the Federal Reserve is completely insulated from politics — it is not. The Federal Reserve system was created by Congress, and Congress can limit the Federal Reserve's freedom if it strays too far from an acceptable path. However, we should point out that the seven members of the Federal Reserve Board are appointed to 14-year terms. The chairman has a four-year guarantee at the helm. The closest analogy is the Supreme Court — members of both institutions righteously consider themselves "above politics," and both institutions from time to time make very unpopular decisions. In the final analysis, the Federal Reserve is the only entity able to (knowingly) risk a full-blown recession to effectively counter accelerating inflation.

THE FEDERAL RESERVE HAS TWO MAJOR FUNCTIONS ASIDE FROM ITS ATTEMPT TO MEET LONG-TERM GOALS

The U.S. central bank has two additional agendas aside from its major goals. The first is its role as "lender of last resort" — the Federal Reserve is the ultimate backstop for the U.S. banking system. The second priority is to stand guard against severe currency depreciation. Beyond a certain point, it simply does not allow the "printing of money" to pay for economic ills. If monetary stringency sometimes results in high interest rates and recessions, so be it. Of course, this was not always the case. Prior to the 1950s, the Federal Reserve routinely purchased securities directly from the Treasury to unabashedly support the government bond market. For most of the 1960s and 1970s, the Federal Reserve was content to "lean against the wind" — tightening credit a bit when the economy overheated, but quickly loosening when activity slowed. This business of risking recessions is fairly new, but should be factored in by those attempting to forecast and invest.

OPEN MARKET OPERATIONS ARE THE MOST IMPORTANT MONETARY POLICY TOOL

As for the tools of monetary policy, the first — open market operations — is by far the most important. These days, Wall Street follows the Federal Reserve's purchases and sales of securities very closely. At the simplest level, an outright purchase of securities in the open market adds reserves to the banking system. An outright sale drains reserves. To see how it works, let us follow a Federal Reserve purchase *(Fig. 20-5)*. In the modern era, banking assets consist primarily of loans and government securities. The majority of their liabilities are demand deposits (checking accounts) and certificates of deposit (CDs). When the Federal Reserve buys a Treasury issue from a bank, it pays by crediting that bank's reserve account at the Fed. The bank now has money available to support a new loan if it wishes. New loans mean new deposits. Moreover, since M1 (the narrowest measure of the money supply) is defined as demand deposits plus currency in circulation, new deposits mean new money. In effect, the Federal Reserve

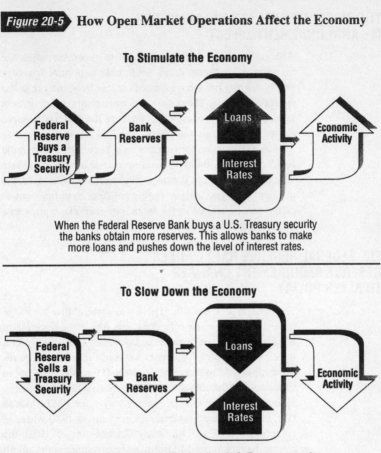

Figure 20-5 **How Open Market Operations Affect the Economy**

creates money by deciding to increase its portfolio holdings of securities. In theory, interest rates decline. If the "supply" of money increases, the "price" of money — the interest rate — falls. Viewed another way, the Federal Reserve, by reducing the "supply" of bonds trading in the market, causes their prices to rise. Because price is inversely proportional to yield, interest rates drop.

THE DISCOUNT RATE IS IMPORTANT FOR ITS ANNOUNCEMENT EFFECT

Although a great deal of publicity is generated when the discount rate is changed, it is not terribly important. In recent years, this rate has been adjusted far less frequently than the federal funds rate. The only reason a discount rate adjustment receives so much attention is because the Federal Reserve makes a public announcement. The Fed can induce exactly the same change in interest rates by a more subtle shift in the funds rate. Thus, the only real importance of a discount rate announcement is that it attracts big headlines. Moreover, the discount rate is actually a lagging indicator of policy — most of the time, changes in the funds rate take place prior to a discount rate shift.

THE FEDERAL RESERVE RARELY USES RESERVE REQUIREMENT CHANGES TO ALTER POLICY

The Federal Reserve's third policy tool, the ability to change bank reserve requirements, is far less important since major adjustments are rarely made. In December 1990, the Federal Reserve's Board of Governors lowered the reserve requirement applicable to some (non-personal) time deposits and to Eurocurrency liabilities, but this was the first time that reserve requirements were changed in any way since 1983. Prior to that, the Fed altered reserve requirements in 1980 when, in compliance with the Monetary Control Act of 1980, the central bank imposed uniform reserve requirements on all commercial banks. Since this policy tool is rarely used, we will not pursue the topic further. Investors should focus attention on the federal funds rate which is primarily determined by open market operations. Since 1982, adjusting the funds rate has been the Fed's main policy lever. Later on, we discuss how the Federal Reserve Bank of New York's "open market desk" — the central bank's trading arm — darts in and out of the reserves market to control this key short-term rate.

BY PEGGING THE FUNDS RATE, THE FEDERAL RESERVE EFFECTIVELY DETERMINES ALL SHORT-TERM INTEREST RATES

What is so important about the federal funds rate? As it is only one interest rate among many, why should traders and investors care whether the funds rate rises or falls? Market participants care because almost all short-term U.S. interest rates are priced off of federal funds *(Fig. 20-6)*. Essentially, the funds rate is the bank's marginal borrowing rate. Banks constantly create liabilities to finance new loans. One such way is to issue CDs. If for some bizarre reason the CD rate is 8% and federal funds are 6%, the banks bypass the former and borrow at the latter. This action alone is sufficient to drive down CD rates. Other rates are linked as well. Take, for example, the prime rate — the rate banks charge their best corporate customers. It

Figure 20-6 **Federal Funds Versus Selected Short Rates**

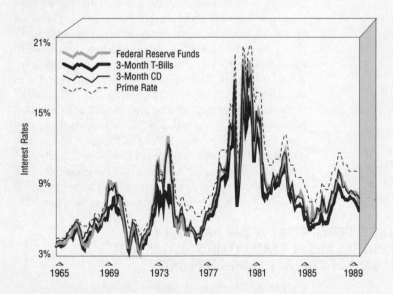

turns out that the banks add about 2% to the CD rate to determine the prime. Therefore, since banks fund a large portion of their loans with CDs, an adjustment here means a change in the prime rate. There are other examples; also linked to federal funds are rates on Treasury bills, commercial paper, bankers acceptances, money market rates, and Euro-dollars. The point is that the funds rate is pivotal, as it affects virtually all other short-term instruments.

LONG-TERM INTEREST RATES DEPEND LARGELY ON INFLATIONARY EXPECTATIONS

Unfortunately, the analysis becomes more complicated if we attempt to link the money markets with long-term securities. Since the relationship is less then perfect, we must think of them as two distinct entities. By definition, short-term securities mature in one year or less. As a result, expectations concerning inflation are not terribly important. How bad can inflation get during the next three to six months? The risk of owning these securities essentially rests with your assumptions regarding near-term Federal Reserve policy. This is not necessarily true of long-term bonds. Inflationary expectations play a much larger role, as future inflation rates must be discounted over a longer time horizon. Consequently, even though the Federal Reserve may be easing, lower short rates may not always drive down long rates *(Fig. 20-7)*. The reason for this is that stronger economic growth can lead to increased borrowing by corporations and consumers. As borrowers come to the credit markets looking to finance a new factory or obtain a home loan, bond market rates can actually rise! But let us not get carried away here — if the Federal Reserve is *aggressively* easing or tightening credit, bond yields will certainly move in the same direction as short-term rates.

THE FEDERAL RESERVE CAN PRECISELY CONTROL SHORT-TERM INTEREST RATES, BUT IT CANNOT CONTROL LONG-TERM RATES

The Federal Reserve controls short-rates through its ability to set the price of reserves — the federal funds rate. But it does not directly control long-term rates. These long-term rates are market-determined and are based on a variety of factors, such as inflation, supply and demand conditions, the credit risk of

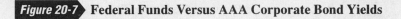

Figure 20-7 Federal Funds Versus AAA Corporate Bond Yields

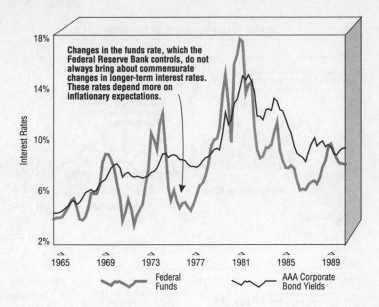

Changes in the funds rate, which the Federal Reserve Bank controls, do not always bring about commensurate changes in longer-term interest rates. These rates depend more on inflationary expectations.

Interest Rates

18%

14%

10%

6%

2%

1965   1969   1973   1977   1981   1985   1989

———— Federal Funds   ——— AAA Corporate Bond Yields

a particular security, and so forth. Nevertheless, knowing which way the Fed will move next is extremely valuable to those investing in a variety of financial markets.

THE FEDERAL RESERVE'S ACTION ALSO AFFECTS THE FOREIGN EXCHANGE MARKET

In addition to the money and bond markets, two more are affected by changes in the federal funds rate — the foreign exchange and equity markets. By its control of short-term interest rates, the Federal Reserve has some degree of influence over the U.S. dollar. Generally speaking, higher rates tend to boost the currency, as global investors seek the highest possible yield. Rising U.S. rates, relative to foreign rates, tend to encourage investment in dollar-denominated assets. When U.S. rates are declining relative to those overseas, investment flows toward other countries and other currencies.

Figure 20-8 indicates the historical relationship between interest rate spreads and the value of the U.S. dollar in

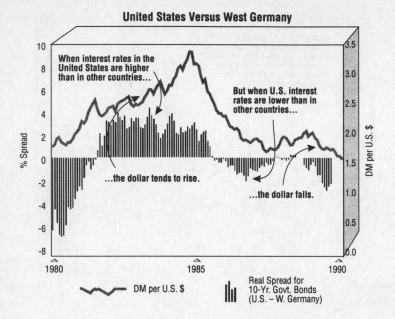

Figure 20-8 Rate Spreads Between the United States and Other Countries Can Have an Impact on the Dollar

United States Versus West Germany

Deutschemark terms. In this example, notice that as the spread narrows, the dollar weakens and vice versa. This raises an obvious question: "Does the Federal Reserve attempt to peg the exchange rate?" Not really. Over the years, the Federal Reserve has consistently formulated interest rate policies that favor domestic concerns. Only in extreme cases does the dollar take first priority. Remember, the central bank really has only one tool — interest rates — with which to influence domestic demand, prices, economic activity, and employment. When push comes to shove, these domestic factors take precedence over imports and exports.

STOCK PRICES ARE ALSO INFLUENCED BY FEDERAL RESERVE POLICY CHANGES

Stock market valuations are also dependent to some extent upon the level and direction of interest rates. Think of stocks the same way you would long-term bonds. Equity prices are a function of the present discounted value of future income streams. If rates decline, future earnings are "discounted" less — the present value moves higher. Alternatively, think of short-term rates as the "opportunity cost" of being in the equity market. For instance, if XYZ corporation pays a 3% dividend while a money market fund pays 9%, the opportunity cost of XYZ ownership is 6%. In order to break even, XYZ's price must rise by 6%. If short rates are 5%, the stock price need only advance 2% for an investor to be satisfied. Of course, beyond these simple examples lies more complexity — in many cases, stock prices and interest rates are *not* inversely correlated. As *Figure 20-9* shows, stock prices can sometimes rise right along with interest rates. It really comes down to whether profit gains outpace rate increases. In the worst case (stagflation), poor earnings trot alongside higher rates. In this environment, you can bet the DOW is headed south. The best case occurs as the economy is coming out of recession — stocks are cheap, earnings are beginning to pick up, and interest rates are low. In this situation, you can bet the farm on higher equity prices. The bottom line is, if the outlook for corporate profits rises, the stock market usually follows *(Fig. 20-10)*.

Figure 20-9 ▶ **S&P 500 Versus Three-Month CD Interest Rate**

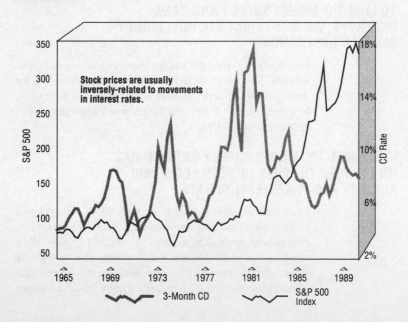

Figure 20-10 How the S&P 500 Tracks Corporate Profits

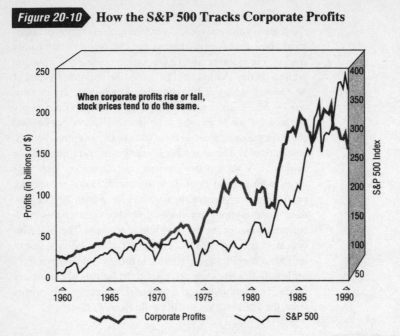

TO LINK THE MONEY SUPPLY AND BANK RESERVES, WE MUST FIRST SEE HOW MONEY AFFECTS THE ECONOMY

Previously, we noted the linkage between reserves and interest rates. Now we examine the link between reserves and the money supply. In order to build a framework for discussion, however, we need to see how the monetary aggregates influence output and prices.

HISTORICALLY, MONEY SUPPLY GROWTH HAS INFLUENCED THE PACE OF BOTH ECONOMIC ACTIVITY AND THE INFLATION RATE

In the good old days — prior to the early 1980s — there was a respectable relationship between the growth rate of nominal GNP and the nominal aggregates M1 and M2. *Figure 20-11* suggests that if the Federal Reserve were able to regulate money growth, it should have reasonable control over the rate of economic expansion. Similarly, *Figure 20-12* compares

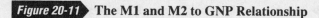

Figure 20-11 The M1 and M2 to GNP Relationship

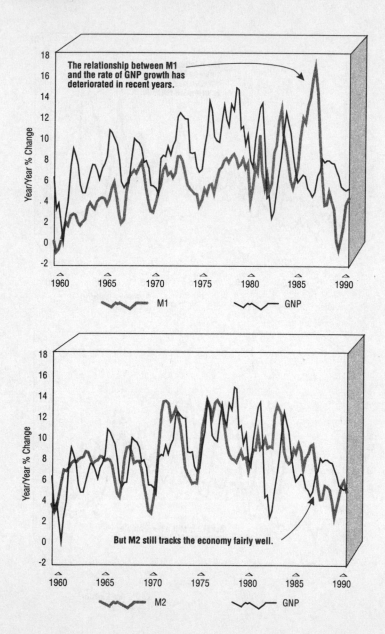

Figure 20-12 **The M1 and M2 to Inflation Relationship**

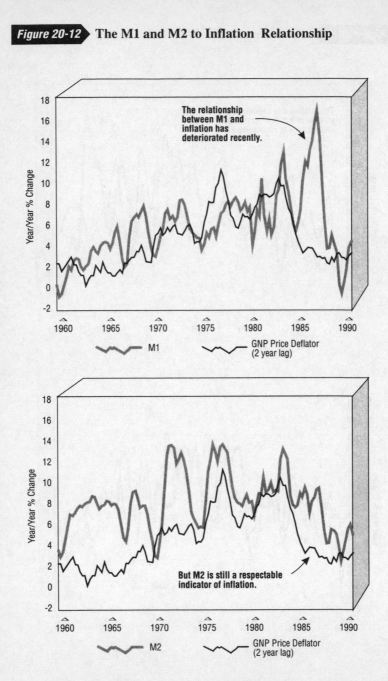

the rate of money growth and inflation two years later. Here again, money growth seems to have some impact on the inflation rate, but with a considerable lag.

THESE RELATIONSHIPS HAVE BECOME LESS CLEAR IN RECENT YEARS

However, these relationships have become less impressive since the mid-1980s. While everyone seems to have an opinion on the subject, we believe the major turning point was the Monetary Control Act of 1980. Among other things, this act phased out Regulation Q. As interest rate ceilings on deposits were lifted, rapid growth of "near money" took place. Innovations, such as money market deposit accounts, allowed depositors to earn interest on bank balances. The net result was a blurring of what "money" actually meant. Was it cash? Or was it savings?

NEVERTHELESS, THE FEDERAL RESERVE STILL TRIES TO TARGET MONEY GROWTH

But old habits are hard to kick. The Federal Reserve continues to target money growth rates, believing that some sort of relationship to GNP still exists. Given this premise, the Fed attempts to regulate the pace of money expansion in order to move toward its ultimate objective of stable, non-inflationary economic growth. The central bank does not have much room for error. If money expands too slowly, the economy will not have sufficient liquidity to grow at the desired pace. If money expands too rapidly, the result will be a pickup in the rate of inflation. In short, the rate of money growth remains a key element in the conduct of monetary policy.

THE RELATIONSHIP BETWEEN REAL M2 AND REAL GNP STILL WORKS WELL

Luckily, there is one money/GNP relationship that still works fairly well. *Figure 20-13* plots real M2 against real GNP. Notice that in many instances, M2 growth bottoms out at the same time as GNP growth. On the way down, M2 seems to lead output by about 12 months. A number of economists use this relationship as a GNP forecasting tool. But the basic problem is still with us — how should we define money?

Figure 20-13 ▶ Real M2 Versus Real GNP

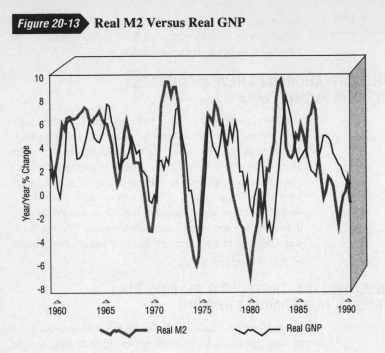

WHAT IS MONEY?

M1 INCLUDES ANYTHING THAT CAN BE USED TO CARRY OUT TRANSACTIONS

Virtually all economists agree that money represents anything that can be used to carry out transactions *(Fig. 20-14)*. Such a definition certainly includes currency and travelers checks. It also includes a variety of checkable deposits, since most businesses accept payment in the form of a check. These checkable deposits consist primarily of demand deposits, NOW accounts and credit union drafts. The items noted above are all included in a measure of money the Federal Reserve refers to as M1.

M2 STARTS WITH M1 AND ADDS OTHER VERY LIQUID ASSETS

There are alternate ways, however, of holding liquid assets. These other assets can be accessed quickly, although in many cases cannot be used directly as means of payment. The Federal Reserve has lumped M1 together with a variety

Figure 20-14 **The Components of M1**

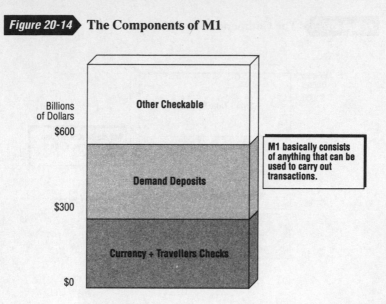

Billions
of Dollars

$600

Other Checkable

Demand Deposits

M1 basically consists
of anything that can be
used to carry out
transactions.

$300

Currency + Travellers Checks

$0

of these instruments into a broader definition of money it calls
M2 *(Fig. 20-15)*. Passbook savings deposits fall into this
category, as do small denomination CDs. Money market
mutual fund shares (MMMFs) at brokerage houses, and money
market deposit accounts (MMDAs) at banks and thrifts are also
incorporated into M2. These two definitions of money, M1
and M2, are by far the most common, even though the Federal
Reserve has an even broader measure it calls M3 *(Fig. 20-16)*.

IT IS NOT ENTIRELY CLEAR WHICH MONETARY
AGGREGATE IS MOST IMPORTANT

The most important point is that there is no clear-cut definition of money. In many cases, only minute differences exist
between the various types of financial instruments; whether
a particular asset should be included in M1 or M2 is not
always obvious. This has bothered economists and policymakers for years. For example, how should the Federal
Reserve respond when M1 and M2 provide entirely different
pictures of money growth? Of economic growth? Of inflation? These problems are not likely to disappear in the near
future. In the meantime, much to the chagrin of "monetarists,"
monetary policy relies heavily upon the judgment of Federal
Reserve officials. ✦

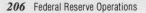

Figure 20-15 The Components of M2

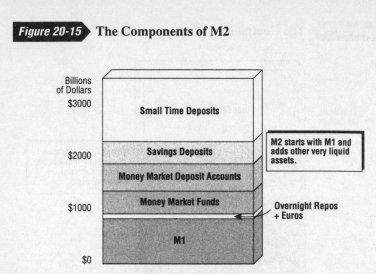

Figure 20-16 The Components of M3

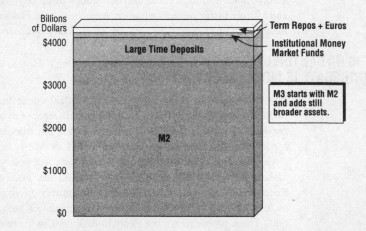

21

Implementation of Federal Reserve Policy

Tricky, but Necessary to Know

s we see it, the implementation of Federal Reserve policy is a four-step process which is summarized in *Figure 21-1*. This chapter explains each step in detail.

STEP 1. ESTABLISH TARGETS FOR THE VARIOUS Ms

As noted above, the Federal Reserve has developed a number of different monetary measures — each of which presumably bears some relationship to the level of economic activity. The first step in the policy process is to identify the linkages between the various monetary aggregates and nominal GNP growth and to specify an annual "target" growth range for M2 and M3. Then the Federal Reserve can calculate reserve levels that it believes will be consistent with achieving the monetary aggregates objectives.

SPECIFYING THE ANNUAL TARGET RANGES IS ITSELF A THREE-STEP PROCESS

First, the Federal Reserve decides upon a desired growth rate for real GNP and an "acceptable" rate of inflation to determine the target rate for expansion of nominal GNP *(Fig. 21-2)*. For example, long-term sustainable growth of real GNP appears to be about 2.5%. If the Federal Reserve decides that it wants to reduce the inflation rate to, say, 2.0%, the desired or targeted rate of nominal GNP growth would be approximately 4.5%.

Next, the Fed compares the historical growth rates of nominal GNP to the growth rate of money to determine the proper relationship between the two. This relationship is know as "velocity." The Federal Reserve has concluded that, over a long period of time, nominal GNP grows at about the same pace as M2. Thus, in this example, given desired nominal GNP growth of 4.5%, M2 should grow at approximately the same 4.5% pace to achieve the desired objective.

Finally, the Fed establishes a band on either side to obtain its target range. Currently, the targets are 2.5%-6.5% for M2 and 1.0%-5.0% for M3. (Note: in the past, the Federal Reserve

 How the Federal Reserve Bank Implements Monetary Policy

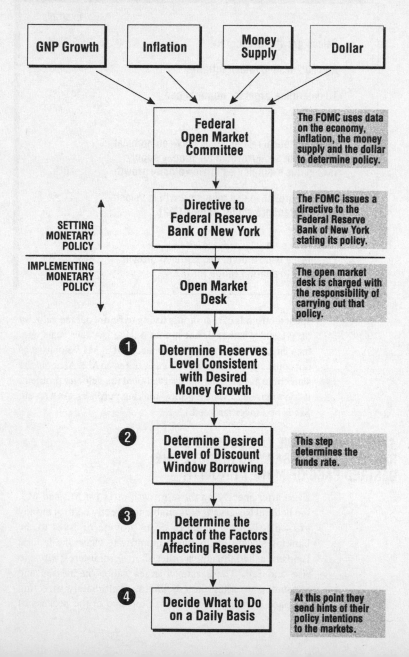

GNP Growth **Inflation** **Money Supply** **Dollar**

Federal Open Market Committee

The FOMC uses data on the economy, inflation, the money supply and the dollar to determine policy.

Directive to Federal Reserve Bank of New York

The FOMC issues a directive to the Federal Reserve Bank of New York stating its policy.

SETTING MONETARY POLICY

IMPLEMENTING MONETARY POLICY

Open Market Desk

The open market desk is charged with the responsibility of carrying out that policy.

❶ **Determine Reserves Level Consistent with Desired Money Growth**

❷ **Determine Desired Level of Discount Window Borrowing**

This step determines the funds rate.

❸ **Determine the Impact of the Factors Affecting Reserves**

❹ **Decide What to Do on a Daily Basis**

At this point they send hints of their policy intentions to the markets.

Figure 21-2 How To Establish Monetary Aggregate Target Bands

	Example
1. Select **growth rate** for GNP	2 1/2%
And add desired rate of **inflation**	2 %
To determine target for **nominal GNP**	41/2%
2. Using historical relationships between nominal GNP growth and growth in the money supply (M2 in this example), estimate **velocity growth**	0%
Nominal growth in GNP minus growth in velocity equals **target growth for money (M2)**	41/2%
3. Establish a band around this targeted growth rate to form a **target range for M2**	21/2% – 61/2%

spent thousands of man-hours trying to figure out the velocity of M1 and whether or not it was "stable." A few years ago, the central bank gave up and conceded that M1 velocity was not constant after all; it now concentrates on M2. At about the same time as the Federal Reserve noted the velocity problem, it "downgraded" M1 for policy-making purposes. As a result, M1 is no longer targeted.)

STEP 2. DETERMINE THE VOLUME OF RESERVES NECESSARY TO ACHIEVE THE DESIRED PACE OF MONEY GROWTH

Even after specifying these growth rates for M2 and M3, the Federal Reserve is still unable to directly control money growth. All it can hope to do is provide reserves to the banking system in sufficient quantity to cause the federal funds rate, and thus most other short-term interest rates, to rise and fall. These rate changes cause businesses and consumers to alter their behavior—ultimately affecting the pace of money expansion. Step two in the process of implementing monetary policy, therefore, is to determine the volume of reserves consistent with achieving the desired pace of monetary growth.

TOTAL RESERVES CONSIST OF BOTH "REQUIRED" AND "EXCESS" RESERVES

"REQUIRED RESERVES" REPRESENT THE AMOUNT OF RESERVES THAT BANKS ARE REQUIRED TO HOLD

At present, the banking system operates in a world of (almost) contemporaneous reserve accounting (CRA). Avoiding the gory details, CRA implies the following: every other Wednesday, the banks must come up with their *required reserves* based on the amount of deposits held. Currently, the average reserve requirement on transaction-type deposits is around 10%; 3% on the first $41.1 million and 12% on anything over that amount. Therefore, by specifying growth targets for money, the Federal Reserve effectively determines desired levels of deposits. By working backward, it can calculate the levels of required reserves that are consistent with achieving both the desired deposit levels and the targeted rates of money growth.

"EXCESS RESERVES" REPRESENT THE ADDITIONAL RESERVES THAT BANKS WANT TO HOLD

While the levels of required reserves provide the link between reserves and money, the Federal Reserve is actually more interested in total reserves which represents the total amount of reserves that the banking system demands. Required reserves can be held either in a special reserve account at the Federal Reserve, or in the form of vault cash. Every business day, the central bank sends each bank a statement indicating its reserve account balance from the previous day. As the maintenance period progresses from Thursday through Wednesday (two weeks hence), the bank is able to monitor its reserve account and compare its balance to its requirements. If the bank is running behind, it can purchase additional reserves from other banks in the federal funds market. Conversely, if it has surplus balances, it sells those in the funds market. On the final day of the two-week period, the bank has 13 days (e.g., Thursday, the 1st through

Tuesday, the 13th) of data from its reserve account on hand. It then makes an estimate of the reserve account balance on the 14th day. A prudent banker does not want to risk falling short in the reserve account because he or she estimated erroneously the reserve balance on that final Wednesday. As a result, each individual bank wants to hold reserves above and beyond the required amount. Those additional balances are called *excess reserves.* The sum of required reserves and excess reserves is called *total reserves (Fig. 21-3).* It represents the total demand for reserves by the banking system — the amount that is required to be held, plus the small amount of additional reserves that banks want to hold.

THE FEDERAL RESERVE NEVER PROVIDES THE BANKING SYSTEM WITH ALL THE RESERVES IT NEEDS THROUGH ITS OPEN MARKET OPERATIONS — IT FORCES SOME TO BORROW AT THE DISCOUNT WINDOW

If the Federal Reserve desired, it could supply the banking system with all the reserves that banks need. But, in doing so, it loses control over the funds rate. In this situation, funds

Figure 21-3 Calculating Net Free Reserves and Net Borrowed Reserves

The Key Equations:

			Example			
TR = **RR** + **ER**			40,000	=	39,000 + 1,000	
NBR = **RR** + **ER** − **DWB**			39,700	=	39,000 + 1,000 − 300	
NFR or **NTB** = **ER** − **DWB**			700	=	1,000 − 300	
(+)	(−)					

Where:

TR	=	Total Reserves
RR	=	Required Reserves
ER	=	Excess Reserves
NBR	=	Non-borrowed Reserves
DWB	=	Discount Window Borrowings
NFR	=	Net Free Reserves
NTB	=	Net Borrowed Reserves

could trade at 2% or 20% — there are simply no constraints. To avoid potentially large swings in the funds rate, the Fed deliberately withholds some of the reserves that the banking system needs. This forces some banks to borrow the necessary reserves from the discount window and ensures that, toward the end of the two-week period, the funds rate will rise at least as high as the discount rate. For example, in the middle of a maintenance period, funds could trade at 6% with a discount rate of 8%. But if the banking system as a whole does not have an adequate quantity of reserves, individual banks soon begin to feel the shortage. Because of a natural tendency to avoid borrowing from the discount window (repeated borrowing brings out the Federal Reserve's auditors) some banks have to aggressively bid for needed reserves, placing upward pressure on the funds rate. Should the funds rate rise far above the discount rate, banks will eventually drop out of the funds market and get the necessary reserves from the Fed's discount window. This mechanism establishes an effective upper and lower limit on the funds rate. By deliberately shortchanging the banking system, and not supplying all of the necessary reserves via open market operations, the central bank establishes a degree of control over the federal funds rate.

KEY POINT:

» **The Federal Reserve Bank never provides all the reserves the banking system needs through its open market operations.**

» **By deliberately short-changing the banking system, the Federal Reserve establishes some control over the funds rate.**

THE FEDERAL RESERVE ACTUALLY TARGETS "NON-BORROWED RESERVES" — TOTAL RESERVES MINUS DISCOUNT WINDOW BORROWINGS

If we subtract the desired amount of discount window borrowing from total reserves, we obtain a reserve aggregate known as "non-borrowed reserves." It is this aggregate that the Federal Reserve Bank is attempting to control (*Fig. 21-3*).

"NET FREE (OR BORROWED) RESERVES" MEASURES ALMOST THE SAME THING

We should point out that at the close of a two-week maintenance period, the level of required reserves is virtually known
(data for 13 of the 14 days is already available). Thus, the only
two items that can change are excess reserves and discount
window borrowings. This means that one important clue to
Federal Reserve policy is the difference between excess
reserves and borrowings. This difference is known as "net
borrowed" or "net free reserves" (again, see *Fig. 21-3*). If the
difference is positive, i.e., excess reserves are greater than
borrowings, it is called *net free reserves*. If borrowings are
larger than excess reserves, it is called *net borrowed reserves*.
Net free and net borrowed reserves are exactly the same thing —
the only difference is whether the difference is a positive or a
negative one. If we focus exclusively on non-borrowed reserves, it is difficult to detect changes in policy because of the
fluctuation in required reserves. However, net free or net
borrowed reserves normally remain constant unless the Federal Reserve changes policy.

On many occasions, the Fed has changed policy by
altering the amount of borrowings from the discount window.
If reserves are ample, the funds rate can be expected to trade
close to the discount rate *(Fig 21-4)*. However, the Federal
Reserve always gets some discount window borrowings because
a few banks invariably overdraw their reserve account and are
forced to the window. In practice, $100 million is generally
considered to be the minimum (frictional) level of borrowing.

IN ADDITION TO THE FUNDS RATE, ANOTHER GAUGE OF FEDERAL RESERVE POLICY IS THE LEVEL OF DISCOUNT WINDOW BORROWINGS

If the Federal Reserve wishes to ease further, and if borrowings are already at very low levels, the central bank cannot
reduce the level of borrowing — the only alternative is to
lower the discount rate. But normally, the Fed initiates an
easing move by first reducing the desired level of discount
window borrowing. If borrowings decline from, say $600
million to $400 millon, the banking system is short fewer
reserves than had been the case previously. Instead of with-
holding $600 million of necessary reserves from the banking
system, the Federal Reserve is now shortchanging it by only

Figure 21-4 Federal Funds Versus Discount Rate

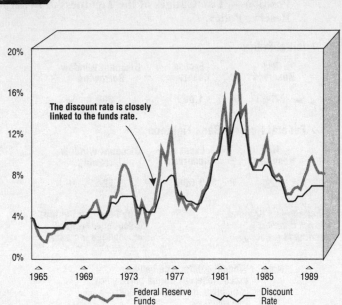

The discount rate is closely linked to the funds rate.

Federal Reserve Funds   Discount Rate

$400 million. As the relative degree of "shortness" declines, the funds rate falls. Conversely, the Fed may tighten policy by increasing the level of discount window borrowings, which causes the funds rate to rise.

WE CAN ALSO GAUGE FEDERAL RESERVE POLICY BY THE NET RESERVES POSITION

As the Federal Reserve tightens, borrowings increase — causing the net reserves position to move from net free reserves, to zero, to progressively deeper levels of net borrowed reserves. The larger the negative number, the tighter the policy is, and the higher the funds rate is relative to the discount rate *(Fig. 21-5)*. When the central bank is in the process of easing, the level of borrowings declines and net borrowed reserves become less deep — the funds rate falls. Thus, the two key measures of Fed policy are discount window borrowings and the net reserves position. In practice, most professional "Fed-watchers" routinely monitor both, because there are occasions when either measure individually can be distorted.

Figure 21-5 Discount Window Borrowings and the Net Reserves Position — Two Gauges of the Tightness of Federal Reserve Policy.

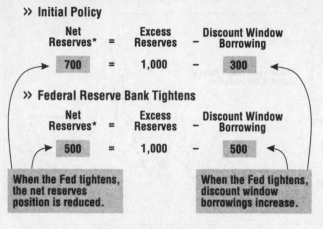

» Initial Policy

Net Reserves*	=	Excess Reserves	−	Discount Window Borrowing
700	=	1,000	−	300

» Federal Reserve Bank Tightens

Net Reserves*	=	Excess Reserves	−	Discount Window Borrowing
500	=	1,000	−	500

When the Fed tightens, the net reserves position is reduced.

When the Fed tightens, discount window borrowings increase.

*Note: When the difference between excess reserves minus borrowings is positive, it is known as "net free reserves."

EVERY $100 MILLION INCREASE IN DISCOUNT WINDOW BORROWING IMPLIES A ¼% RISE IN THE FUNDS RATE, AND VICE VERSA

The above discussion suggests that there should be some relationship between the funds rate/discount rate spread and the targeted level of net borrowed reserves. Unfortunately, the linkage is not airtight. There are a number of technical factors that can affect the level of reserves. If these factors collectively drain (or supply) reserves, the funds rate is subject to some upward (or downward) pressure. Also, banks' demand for excess reserves can fluctuate over time which causes net borrowed reserves to change. Nevertheless, despite all of these potential difficulties, a rule of thumb that works reasonably well is to assume that a change in the Federal Reserve's net borrowed reserves target of $100 million causes a change in the funds rate of 20-25 basis points. Thus, a shift from $600 million to $400 million of net borrowed reserves causes the funds rate to fall 40-50 basis points.

CHANGES IN THE FUNDS RATE ARE IMPORTANT BECAUSE MONETARY POLICY WORKS THROUGH CHANGES IN INTEREST RATES

How do all these changes in reserves affect the rate of money growth? The answer is that the mechanism works entirely through changes in interest rates. As the Federal Reserve tightens, the funds rate rises — prompting all short-term rates (including the prime) to rise and discouraging individuals and corporations from borrowing. The reduction in loan demand causes a slowdown in deposit creation, thereby slowing money growth.

THE FEDERAL RESERVE TRIES TO REGULATE ECONOMIC GROWTH BY ALTERING THE LEVEL OF DISCOUNT WINDOW BORROWING

Summing up, the Fed attempts to regulate money growth by altering the level of discount window borrowings and net borrowed reserves. This gives rise to changes in interest rates, which ultimately have an impact on the demand for money. It should be pointed out that the linkages in the process are quite loose, and furthermore, the mechanism works with a lag. The Federal Reserve simply does not have the ability to control money growth with a high degree of precision. But if the Fed forces interest rates high enough, economic activity slows along with money growth. If the central bank allows rates to slide, eventually the economy and money growth begin to rebound.

STEP 3. THE CENTRAL BANK MUST CONTEND WITH A VARIETY OF FACTORS THAT CAN CAUSE RESERVE LEVELS TO FLUCTUATE

As mentioned above, the Federal Reserve tries to indirectly regulate money growth by changing the level of net free or net borrowed reserves. But once a target level is established, there are additional problems — other factors affect the level of reserves in any given week. If the Fed looks the other way, the funds rate can fluctuate wildly as the combined effect of the factors swing about. For instance, let us say certain technical factors are about to drain $1 billion of reserves during a one-week period. If the Fed does not intervene, the funds rate surges as the reserves shortage is translated into more aggressive bidding for available funds. Ultimately, discount window borrowings will increase by the same $1 billion because the banking system cannot obtain the necessary reserves elsewhere. If the operating factors then turn around the next week and provide $1 billion of reserves, the funds rate plummets along with discount window borrowings. To avoid these disruptive gyrations, the Federal Reserve offsets the effects of these factors through open market operations. If the operating factors drain $1 billion of reserves, the Fed will attempt to add $1 billion via open market operations, and vice versa.

THERE ARE MANY FACTORS AFFECTING RESERVES

These so-called "operating factors" are all items on the Federal Reserve's balance sheet apart from its own holdings of securities and reserve balances. There are 15 of these factors, but only four will be discussed — currency in circulation, float, Treasury deposits, and foreign central bank deposits.

CURRENCY IN CIRCULATION IS PROBABLY THE EASIEST TO UNDERSTAND

The easiest factor to explain is "currency in circulation." As individuals cash checks, a bank will eventually need to obtain additional currency. To do so, it goes to its local Federal Reserve Bank and "pays" for it by drawing upon its reserve account balance. Therefore, changes in currency affect the level of bank reserves *(Fig. 21-6)*. For instance, during the December holidays, we all run to our automatic teller machines for cash. This has the effect of reducing reserves in the banking system which must be put back via open market operations.

FLOAT IS MORE VOLATILE

Perhaps the most volatile operating factor is "Federal Reserve float." The problem of float usually arises because foul weather or a computer glitch interferes with the normal check clearing process — yet another job handled by the Fed. Essentially, two banks claim credit for a deposit, when in reality only one deposit was made. To understand this, assume that, for whatever reason, there is a delay from the time Bank A's reserve account at the Fed is increased and when Bank B's

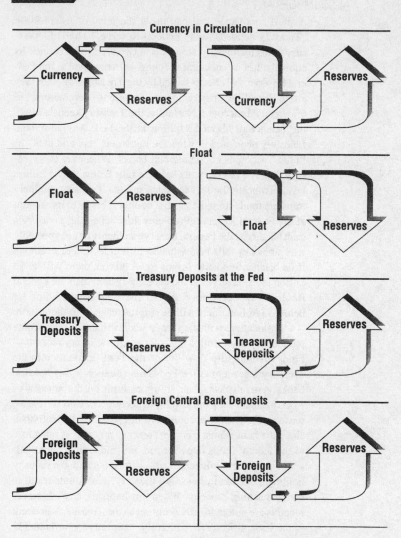

Figure 21-6 Impact on Reserves of Various Factors

account is reduced. For a while, both banks actually hold the same deposit — and thus the reserves. During this delay, reserves are temporarily increased by a rise in float. In response, the Fed steps in and removes the surplus reserves.

THE TREASURY'S CASH BALANCE IS
ALSO IMPORTANT

A third annoyance that can upset the level of reserves are "Treasury deposits at the Federal Reserve." The U.S. Treasury holds its funds (your taxes) in two types of accounts. Its equivalent of a "checking account" is maintained at the Federal Reserve. All checks issued by the Treasury, whether they are to Social Security recipients or defense contractors, are drawn on this account. Normally, the Treasury keeps a working balance of about $5 billion at the Fed. Any additional funds are deposited in what are known as "tax and loan" or "TT&L" accounts at commercial banks. Whenever the Treasury makes a payment, its balance falls below the $5 billion level. To bring the balance back up, the Treasury routinely transfers funds from the TT&L accounts at banks to its account at the Federal Reserve. Problems arise when the Treasury's cash balance at the Federal Reserve suddenly or unexpectedly rises above or falls below the $5 billion level. For example, if its balance suddenly surges to $8 billion, there will be $3 billion fewer reserves in the banking system than the Federal Reserve expects. Conversely, if the cash balance dips far below $5 billion, there will be surplus reserves in the system.

Dislocations with the Treasury's cash balance can become particularly acute following a large inflow of tax receipts — funds involuntarily flow out of the TT&L accounts into the Treasury's account at the Fed. This situation arises because banks generally establish an upper limit on the amount of TT&L balances they are willing to accept. They do so for two reasons. First, these accounts are not particularly profitable, since the banks must pay the Treasury an interest rate close to the federal funds rate. Second, tax and loan account balances must be "collateralized" — fully backed by security holdings. Sizable inflows into these TT&L accounts result in banks reaching capacity. When this happens, any additional receipts are automatically remitted to the Treasury's account at the Federal Reserve. Currently, "capacity" is around $32 billion. If, during the height of tax season, the Treasury's total cash balance reached $40 billion (and only $32 billion can be maintained in tax and loan accounts), the remaining $8 billion will reside in the Treasury's Federal Reserve account. Thus, its balance at the Fed is $3 billion higher than normal. The banking system is short that same $3 billion of reserves — reserves that must be replaced by the Fed.

FOREIGN CENTRAL BANKS ALSO HOLD DEPOSITS AT THE FEDERAL RESERVE TO SERVICE THEIR FOREIGN EXCHANGE OPERATIONS

The final operating factor to be discussed is "foreign central bank deposits." Foreign central banks maintain accounts at the Federal Reserve primarily to service their foreign exchange operations. If, for example, the Bank of England purchases dollars, funds are transferred from the overseas branch of a U.S. bank to the U.K. central bank account at the Federal Reserve. This action serves to decrease the level of reserves in the banking system. The Fed quickly attempts to replenish lost reserves, because otherwise, pressures will develop in the federal funds market.

WHAT IS IMPORTANT IS THE NET EFFECT OF ALL THESE FACTORS

These operating factors — currency in circulation, float, Treasury deposits and foreign central bank deposits — are the major ones that affect the level of reserves in any given period. To determine the volume of necessary open market operations (the amount of reserves it must add or drain), the Federal Reserve essentially starts with the level of non-borrowed (or net borrowed) reserves from the prior period and adds the net effect of the operating factors to determine the level of reserves that would be in the system if they did nothing. It then compares this result to the desired or targeted level of non-borrowed (or net borrowed) reserves that was previously determined. The difference between these two figures represents the amount of reserves that the Fed must add or drain via open market operations for that particular two-week maintenance period.

NOW THE FEDERAL RESERVE MUST FIGURE OUT HOW IT IS GOING TO ADD OR DRAIN THE NECESSARY VOLUME OF RESERVES

Once the Federal Reserve calculates the volume of necessary open market operations, how does it actually inject or drain reserves? To supply reserves, the Fed basically has the following four options:

» An outright purchase of securities;
» A purchase internally from a foreign central bank;
» A system repo; or
» A customer repo.

To drain reserves, the Federal Reserve Bank can choose among the following:

» An outright sale of securities;
» A sale internally to a foreign central bank; or
» A reverse repo (matched-sale/purchase agreement).

WHEN THE FEDERAL RESERVE BUYS SECURITIES, IT ADDS RESERVES TO THE SYSTEM *PERMANENTLY*

It is important to understand that when the Federal Reserve purchases securities, either from the "Street" or from a foreign central bank, it is permanently adding reserves to the banking system *(Fig. 21-7)*. This will be important to us later on when we discuss how the Fed actually carries out its day-to-day operations. When the Federal Reserve buys a government security from a dealer, the dealer gives up the security, but in exchange gets a credit to its checking account — and the dealer's bank gains reserves. When the Fed buys a security from a foreign central bank, the process is a bit more circuitous, but the end result is the same.

Figure 21-7 The Federal Reserve Can Add (or Drain) Reserves on Either a Permanent or Temporary Basis

	Permanent	Temporary
A. Add		
1. Outright purchase of securities	✔	
2. Outright purchase of securities from a foreign central bank	✔	
3. System repo		✔
4. Customer repo		✔
B. Drain		
1. Outright sale of securities	✔	
2. Outright sale of securities to a foreign central bank	✔	
3. Reverse repo (matched sale/purchase)		✔

WHEN THE FEDERAL RESERVE DOES A SYSTEM REPO IT ADDS RESERVES ON A *TEMPORARY* BASIS

The mechanics of a "system repo" (or repurchase agreement) are essentially the same, but in this case reserves have temporarily been added to the banking system. The dealer community sells a government security to the Federal Reserve, but with a simultaneous agreement to repurchase it at a later date (at a slightly higher price). These repos can be done on either an overnight basis (one business day), or for a period of time up to seven days depending upon the needs of the Fed. Because system repos are essentially a secured form of dealer borrowing, the rate is normally just under the federal funds rate — the rate that applies to unsecured borrowing.

CUSTOMER REPOS ALSO ADD RESERVES TO THE SYSTEM ON A *TEMPORARY* BASIS

The final method which the Federal Reserve uses to add reserves to the banking system is a "customer repo." The mechanics of a customer repo are nearly identical to that of a system repo. And, as is the case with a system repo, a customer repo temporarily adds reserves to the banking system. Thus, the Federal Reserve has two ways to provide temporary reserves to the banking system. To understand the concept of a customer repo, take another look at the role of foreign central banks. Earlier, we noted that these banks have accounts at the Fed to service their foreign exchange transactions. As intelligent bankers, they recognize that if money sits idle in a deposit account, it earns no interest. Therefore, these banks leave instructions with the Federal Reserve to invest those funds overnight. Normally, the Fed routinely sells them a security out of its own portfolio on an overnight basis, which allows the foreign central bank to earn interest. But the Fed can choose (for reasons we describe in a moment) to let the "Street" sell the foreign central bank the security. In this case, the Federal Reserve arranges a customer repo. We say "arrange" because the Federal Reserve is essentially facilitating a transaction between a dealer and a foreign central bank. If you have always wondered who the "customer" was, now you know — it is a foreign central bank.

WHEN THE FEDERAL RESERVE NEEDS TO DRAIN RESERVES, ITS CHOICES ARE ENTIRELY ANALOGOUS

An outright sale of securities permanently drains reserves from the banking system. A "matched-sale/purchase agreement" (or "reverse repo") drains reserves from the banking system on a temporary basis. The Federal Reserve chooses between these operations in accordance with its needs.

STEP 4. DECIDE WHAT TO DO ON A DAILY BASIS

NEARLY ALL FEDERAL RESERVE OPERATIONS ARE DESIGNED TO OFFSET THE IMPACT OF THE OPERATING FACTORS

Now we are ready to see what the Federal Reserve does on a daily basis. Recall, there are always operating factors adding or draining reserves from the banking system that the Federal Reserve — actually the Federal Reserve Bank of New York's trading "Desk" — attempts to counterbalance with open market operations. In understanding Fed operations, it is crucial to recognize that about 90% of the central bank's actions are designed to do nothing more than offset the impact of the operating factors. If the Fed does repurchase agreements, it is not necessarily signaling an easing of policy. Similarly, reverse repos do not always imply that the Fed is tightening. But from time to time, the Fed *will* use open market operations to signal a policy change. In the discussion that follows we try to give you some hints for separating the wheat from the chaff. We focus on situations in which the Fed must add reserves to the banking system — simply because it is in "add mode" most of the time. But the discussion can just as easily be applied to those situations in which the Fed must drain reserves.

TO DECIDE WHAT TO DO ON ANY GIVEN DAY, THE FEDERAL RESERVE MUST ANTICIPATE RESERVES NEEDS FOUR TO SIX WEEKS IN ADVANCE

IF IT EXPECTS A SIZEABLE ADD NEED FOR AN EXTENDED PERIOD OF TIME, THE FED INJECTS RESERVES TO THE SYSTEM ON A PERMANENT BASIS

If it sees a need to add a sizeable quantity of reserves for an extended period of time, usually an amount in excess of $4 billion per day for four consecutive weeks, the Federal

Reserve will consider an outright purchase of securities *(Fig. 21-8)*. It then buys T-bills or Treasury notes and bonds — called a "bill pass" or "coupon pass" — and adds those securities to its own portfolio. As noted previously, this adds an equivalent amount of reserves to the banking system on a permanent basis. For our purposes, these outright purchases of securities are generally regarded as purely technical operations and have no policy implications. It should be stressed, however, that when discussing Federal Reserve operations, there are no hard and fast rules! The only other point that should be noted here is that these transactions are not done very often, usually only four or five times a year.

IT MIGHT ALSO BUY SOME SECURITIES FROM FOREIGN CENTRAL BANKS

If the Federal Reserve anticipates a somewhat smaller add requirement (that also extends for a number of weeks), it can choose to buy some government securities from a foreign central bank *(Fig. 21-8)*. This adds a more modest amount of reserves to the banking system on a permanent basis. As was the case above, this action is devoid of policy significance.

IF RESERVES NEEDS ARE SMALLER OR LESS PROTRACTED, THE FEDERAL RESERVE ADDS RESERVES ON A TEMPORARY BASIS

More often, however, the Federal Reserve's add requirement varies. It may need to add a large amount of reserves for a week or two, only to be followed by a period in which its

Figure 21-8 How the Federal Reserve Decides What To Do on Any Given Day

A. To Add Reserves	Probable Federal Reserve Action
1. Large and extended need	Bill or coupon pass
2. Small and extended need	Security purchase from foreign central bank
3. Temporary need	System repos and/or customer repos

B. To Drain Reserves	Probable Federal Reserve Action
1. Large and extended need	Bill sale
2. Small and extended need	Security sale to a foreign bank
3. Temporary need	Matched sale/purchase agreement

add requirement shrinks dramatically or even turns into a drain requirement. In these situations, the Fed opts for one of the methods by which it can add reserves to the system temporarily, i.e., system repos (either overnight or multi-day) or customer repos *(Fig. 21-8)*.

IT CAN PROVIDE THE SAME AMOUNT OF TEMPORARY RESERVES IN A NUMBER OF WAYS

At this point, it should be noted that the Federal Reserve can provide exactly the same amount of temporary reserves to the system in a variety of ways *(Fig. 21-9)*. If, for example, it sees a need to inject $2 billion of reserves per day for four consecutive days it can do $2 billion of overnight system repos on each of the four days. Alternatively, it can execute a $2 billion four-day system repo, or it can opt for a $2 billion customer repo on each of the four days. Every one of these operations supply exactly the same amount of reserves.

Figure 21-9 The Federal Reserve Can Provide Exactly the Same Amount of Temporary Reserves to the System in a Variety of Ways

To provide $8 billion of reserves:

1. *$2 billion of overnight RPs on each of four days*

Overnight RPs — Monday	$2
Overnight RPs — Tuesday	$2
Overnight RPs — Wednesday	$2
Overnight RPs — Thursday	$2
	$8

2. *$2 billion of a four-day system repo*

Four-day RPs — Monday ($2 billion x 4)	$8

3. *$2 billion of customer RPs on each of four days*

Customer RPs — Monday	$2
Customer RPs — Tuesday	$2
Customer RPs — Wednesday	$2
Customer RPs — Thursday	$2
	$8

HOWEVER, EACH OF THESE OPERATIONS CONVEYS A VERY DIFFERENT MESSAGE TO THE MARKETS IN TERMS OF POLICY

Overnight system repos are generally considered to be the most aggressive action the Fed can take *(Fig. 21-10)*. They tell the "Street" that the funds rate is at least 25 basis points higher than what the Fed intends. Thus, overnight system repos are frequently indicative of a change in policy. Term (multi-day) repos are usually regarded as technical and imply that the Fed faces a fairly sizeable add requirement. In addition, multi-day system repos indicate that the funds rate may be a bit on the high side, but not high enough to trigger overnight repos. Customer repos indicate a more modest add requirement and are also generally viewed as technical. When the Federal Reserve arranges customer repurchase agreements, the funds rate is relatively in line with their objective.

Figure 21-10 **Each of These Operations Will Convey a Different Message to the Markets**

Message Sent

Overnight Repos Very aggressive, funds rate too high, possible sign of easier policy stance

Term Repos Technical, sizeable add requirement

Customer Repos Technical, smallish add requirement

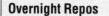

THERE IS NO INHERENT LOGIC IN THE MARKET'S INTERPRETATION OF THESE VARIOUS OPERATIONS

As shown above, there is no inherent logic behind the market's interpretation of these various operations from a purely reserves viewpoint — the Fed can provide exactly the same amount of reserves in any number of different ways. But in the pre-1979 period when the central bank was explicitly targeting the federal funds rate, traders quickly learned that when the Fed executed each of these various operations, it was trying to tell the market something about policy. As a result, the above interpretations became widely accepted. In today's world, even though the Federal Reserve is less explicitly targeting the funds rate, the same connotation has been attached to these various types of repos. The Fed is well aware that the market interprets different operations in different ways, and it uses that to its advantage when it wants to convey a particular policy message.

HOW WILL THE FEDERAL RESERVE CHOOSE BETWEEN THESE VARIOUS OPERATIONS?

Let us see how the Fed might choose between these various methods of providing reserves to the system on a temporary basis. History suggests that the Fed's selection of one operation over another is based on three factors:

» The size of the add requirement;
» The level of the funds rate; and
» The policy message the Fed wants to send.

IF THE ADD NEED IS SIZEABLE, BUT ONLY TEMPORARY, THE FEDERAL RESERVE WILL HAVE TO SELECT SOME SORT OF SYSTEM REPOS

When the add need is sizeable but temporary, the Fed selects some type of system repo because foreign central banks hold a total of only about $5 billion in their accounts. If the Fed needs to add $8 billion of reserves on a given day, it cannot satisfy that reserves need via customer repos. The maximum it can do is $5 billion and, typically, customer repos do not exceed $3 billion. Thus, size becomes one criterion in the decision-making process. In this case, the Federal Reserve will be called upon to execute some type of system repos.

THE CHOICE BETWEEN OVERNIGHT AND TERM REPOS IS MOST LIKELY DETERMINED BY THE LEVEL OF THE FUNDS RATE

As noted above, if funds are 25 basis points higher than the Fed desires, it will probably select overnight repos rather than multi-day repos to signal to the markets that the rate is considerably higher than the central bank intends. If faced with a sizeable add requirement, but the funds rate is less than 25 basis points higher than desired, the central bank most likely will choose multi-day system repos. In each instance, the Fed considers the size of the add requirement, but then looks at the level of the funds rate and picks the operation that best reflects its policy objective.

THE SAME TYPE OF CONSIDERATIONS APPLY
WHEN THE FEDERAL RESERVE IS FACED WITH
A MORE MODEST ADD REQUIREMENT

When the add requirement is modest, the choice is generally between overnight system repos and customer repos. Once again, the Fed examines the level of the funds rate. If it is 25 basis points higher than intended, the Fed most likely opts for overnight system repos to convey the message that the funds rate is on the high side. At a somewhat lower funds rate level, the Fed will probably opt for customer repo. If, for whatever reason, the funds rate is on the low side, even though the central bank needs to add reserves, it may decide not to intervene on that day rather than risk sending the market an inappropriate signal. For example, if the Fed arranges customer repos with the funds rate at a lower level than on other recent days when it did customer repos, the market may erroneously conclude that the Fed is easing. Thus, as has been the case all along, the Fed first looks at the size of its add need, checks the level of the funds rate, and picks the operation that seems most appropriate for the policy it is pursuing at that particular point in time.

IF THE FEDERAL RESERVE WANTS TO CHANGE ITS
POLICY STANCE, IT WILL ALTER THE LEVEL OF
DISCOUNT WINDOW BORROWINGS

If the Federal Reserve looks at the economic situation — GNP growth, employment, inflation, and so forth — and decides that it wants to adopt an easier policy stance, it reduces the amount of discount window borrowings and increases the net reserves level slightly. This means that the central bank must provide more reserves to the market through its open market operations. For instance, if it wants to reduce discount window borrowings by $200 million, then it must add an extra $200 million of reserves via open market operations. This process, presumably, causes the funds rate to trade lower. If the Fed wants to tighten, it boosts the amount of discount window borrowing.

THE FED WILL ALSO WANT TO SEND A SIGNAL TO
THE MARKETS OF AN EASIER POLICY STANCE

To facilitate the transition, the Federal Reserve will want to send a signal of an easier policy stance to the markets. If the add need is sizeable, it may choose overnight repos rather than multi-day repos to convey that message. With a smaller need to supply reserves, it can once again choose overnight system repos rather than a customer repo operation. Occasionally, it will send an easing signal by arranging customer repos with funds at a particularly low level. But the Fed *never* signals a policy change with multi-day repurchase agreements.

TO DETECT A CHANGE IN POLICY, TRY TO DETERMINE WHEN THE FEDERAL RESERVE IS BEING MORE AGGRESSIVE THAN IT HAD BEEN PREVIOUSLY

The key to detecting a change in policy is in determining when the Federal Reserve is being more aggressive than it had been previously for any particular add requirement. The problem is that the Fed has much more accurate data on the actual volume of banking system reserves than is publicly available. Each day it learns what happened to reserves levels on the previous day. Those of us on the "Street" get an update only once a week. If the Fed does something differently than expected, the obvious dilemma that an analyst faces is deciding when the Fed is simply reacting to an unexpected change in one or more of the factors affecting reserves, and when it is trying to signal a policy change.

FIRST, DECIDE IF *YOU* WOULD EASE POLICY

The first thing that a Fed-watcher does is look at the recent economic statistics and decide whether, from his or her viewpoint, a change in policy might be warranted *(Fig. 21-11)*. *Chances are if the analyst would not make a change in policy, the Federal Reserve would not either.*

Figure 21-11 How to Detect Federal Reserve Policy Changes

1. Decide if *you* would change policy.
2. Check for any unusual events.
   A. Bad weather someplace in the country?
   B. Rumors of Federal Reserve intervention in the foreign exchange market?
   C. Shortly after a tax date?
3. Do not reach any conclusion on the basis of a single day's operation.

SECOND, BE ON THE LOOKOUT FOR ANY UNUSUAL EVENTS THAT COULD ALTER RESERVE LEVELS

The second thing the Fed-watcher does is see whether there have been any unusual events that could alter reserves levels. If, for example, the analyst notes that there has been a major snowstorm in the Midwest, he or she would be alerted to the possibility that float could rise and provide more reserves to the banking system. Or the Fed-watcher might have heard that there had been a considerable amount of foreign exchange intervention. (When the Federal Reserve buys foreign currencies, banking system reserves increase.) Or perhaps it is a period shortly after one of the big tax dates when it becomes much more difficult to estimate the level of the Treasury's cash balance at the Fed. If there have been some unusual events taking place, an analyst will be reluctant to conclude that an unexpected action is indicative of a change in policy.

THIRD, NEVER REACH A CONCLUSION ON THE BASIS OF A SINGLE-DAY'S ACTIVITY

One final point: we can rarely reach a conclusion about Federal Reserve policy on the basis of a single day's operation. Generally, all that can be done on that day is to note that this action seemed unusual and could be indicative of a change in policy. We want to track the behavior of the funds rate over the rest of that day, and wait to see some confirmation of an easier policy stance reflected in Fed activity on subsequent days.

ABOUT 90% OF THE FEDERAL RESERVE'S OPEN MARKET OPERATIONS ARE PURELY TECHNICAL

We have seen that about 90% of the Federal Reserve's open market operations are designed to do nothing more than offset the impact of the operating factors. The very fact that the Fed is doing repos or matched sales does not necessarily indicate a policy change. What is important is the level of the funds rate and the particular operation that the central bank selects. Furthermore, it should be understood that the Fed tries very hard not to send misleading signals to the market, although, occasionally, the message that the Federal Reserve thinks it is sending is not the signal that the market receives.

THE REMAINING 10% OF THE TIME, THE FEDERAL RESERVE USES ITS OPEN MARKET OPERATIONS TO SIGNAL A POLICY CHANGE — SO PAY ATTENTION!

Because the Federal Reserve uses open market operations to signal a change in policy about 10% of the time, "surprise" repos or reverses do ring a bell on Wall Street. Since early detection of a policy shift is of supreme importance to the financial markets, the professional Fed-watcher's primary function is knowing *when* to ring the bell. ✦